Setting Up and Running a School Library

Nicola Baird

The VSO ECOE Programme

Heinemann Educational Publishers
Halley Court, Jordan Hill, Oxford OX2 8EJ
a division of Reed Educational & Professional Publishing Ltd

Heinemann: A Division of Reed Publishing (USA) Inc.
361 Hanover Street, Portsmouth, NH 03801-3912, USA

Heinemann Educational Books (Nigeria) Ltd
PMB 5205, Ibadan
Heinemann Educational Boleswa
PO Box 10103, Village Post Office, Garborone, Botswana

MELBOURNE   AUCKLAND
FLORENCE   PRAGUE   MADRID   ATHENS
SINGAPORE   TOKYO   SAO PAULO
CHICAGO   PORTSMOUTH (NH)   MEXICO
IBADAN   GABORONE   JOHANNESBURG
KAMPALA   NAIROBI

VSO
317 Putney Bridge Road
London SW15 2PN

First published by Heinemann Educational Publishers in 1994

British Library Cataloguing in Publication Data
A catalogue record for this book is available from the British Library.

Cover design by Threefold Design

Acknowledgements
The author and publishers are grateful to the following for permission to
reproduce their photographs:

Simon Etherton (**3.1** and **11.1**); Nick Hayward (**1.2**); Liz Platt (**13.2** and **14.1**);
VSO/Jeremy Hartley (**5.1**); VSO/Sol Fidalgo (**13.1**).

ISBN 0435 923048

Phototypeset by PDQ Repro Ltd, Bungay, Suffolk
Printed and bound in Great Britain

96 97 10 9 8 7 6 5 4 3

Contents

Foreword

●●

Setting up and running a school library is one of the most
satisfying jobs a teacher can perform. As a teacher–librarian you
will be able to develop children's love of books and encourage
them to read. This in turn will improve their literacy skills, which
they will enjoy, remember and share long after their school days
are over. You can also show students how to find out information
from the books in the library, and this too is a skill for life. People
need information to educate themselves and develop their true
potential, and for this they need literacy skills and access to books.
The library provides access to books; it is a place where information is shared.

Setting up a library is also a great challenge. It can be hard work, so
it is recommended that you work closely with many other people
at your school. In this way the library will belong to everyone at
the school and can be made to benefit many generations of
students.

This book has been written to help you to set up and run the type
of library that best suits your school. The guidelines are based on
the many years' experience of VSO teachers and librarians working
with local colleagues in low-resource schools throughout the
developing world. Step-by-step instructions are provided to help
you establish the library and run it well. The book presents ideas to
help you harness your colleagues' and students' enthusiasm and to
encourage them to make the idea of their own school library a
reality.

There may be times when you feel setting up a library is a struggle,
but don't despair. The problems you face have been tackled by
other teacher–librarians in similar situations. This book includes
photographs of school libraries around the world; just take a look
at these and remember you are not alone. Make sure you network
with other school librarians and with public and specialist
librarians in your country. Librarians are usually very supportive,
so even if the nearest library is 300 kilometres away it is worth
making contact with the people running it.

Most teachers who are asked to set up and run a library are not
trained librarians – and neither am I. However, the people who
helped plan and write this book with me have direct experience of
setting up a school library in the developing world and/or have
professional library qualifications. Thank you to all of them for

sharing their knowledge – especially Daniel Aidoo, Marie Bray, Liz Doyle, Simon Etherton, Peter Fenton, Nicole Fitton, Maggie Gardiner, Nick Hayward, Renato Masetti, Liz Platt, Jean Playfair and Peter Williams. Thanks also to Penny Amerena, Silke Bernau and Julian Parr at VSO, as well as Andrew Baird, Daniel Clery and Neil Macdonald for computer generosity. Particular thanks go to Gill Harris and Cynthia Stirrup for their professional advice on library procedures.

Nicola Baird

Introduction

What is this book about?

This book explains how teachers can set up and run a successful school library. In it you will find advice and information on how to:

- set up a small library and build bookshelves
- select books for your library
- make a written record of your school's books, pamphlets and other library stock such as newspapers, magazines, audio tapes and videos.
- divide the library stock into subject areas
- choose the best method of letting students borrow library books.
- repair damaged books.

In addition, you will find useful 'teaching tips' throughout the book and, in chapter 16, the addresses of international organisations which may supply free books to your school.

Why do you need to use this book?

If you are planning your school's first library this book will guide you through each step. If your school already has a library this book will help you to ensure its success – but do think carefully before you make any changes. You may not need to make many improvements if the books and other stock are easy to find, if they are in good condition and if people use the library whenever it is open. However, if your library suffers from complicated procedures that are not maintained, if it lacks stock or if it is underused by students (perhaps because they think it is an unfriendly place), then this book will help you. It explains how to improve and simplify your library systems and gives you ideas to encourage students and teachers to use the library.

Organising or re-organising a library can seem complicated. By reading this step-by-step guide you should be able to obtain a clear idea of what needs to be done and why, so that you can explain the importance of library systems to students and teachers who help you. Be prepared for questions like 'Why are we making a library?' or 'Why are we organising the books in this way?' Your answers will encourage people's interest. Remember that a successful library will be used often and by everybody at your school, so the more people you can interest in it the better.

Figure 1.1 A good school library looks friendly and has lots of posters as well as curtains. All these ideas might work well in your library. Study areas are best set up around a table with chairs, but many students prefer mats or comfortable chairs for leisure reading.

How to use this book

The book is divided into chapters. Each chapter gives you a step-by-step explanation of the things to do, and the order in which to do them, to make a well organised library. In each chapter you will find advice on

- what you need to do
- why you need to do it
- how to do it.

There are also comments from volunteers working with VSO (Voluntary Service Overseas) and their national counterparts on their experiences of setting up libraries in primary and secondary schools.

It is recommended that you first read the book through from beginning to end. You will see that some of the procedures involved in organising a library are essential: things you *must* do for success; while others are optional: things you can do to improve the library if you have the time and energy. Think about how these ideas will work at your school, and make sure you discuss your library plans with the head teacher, staff and students. After deciding which systems are appropriate for your library, read the book for a second time. This time use it as a textbook, and start to organise the school library as you read the chapters.

Some words describing library work might be new to you. Selected words are explained at the back of the book in the Key Words section starting on p. 128. Key words are listed alphabetically.

Every school is different. Some schools have enough money to buy new books; some schools have no money to spend on books. This book is written for teachers at schools with very little money. These schools are lucky enough to have teachers like you who want to help their students by making a user-friendly library for them. Good luck!

● ●

Teaching tip

A story about soccer posters

This is the story of a school library that was beautifully organised but that nobody ever used. The librarian just sat at the desk all day in a big room, which was full of books.

It was very boring. She wanted to encourage students to use the books but, whatever she did, the students just didn't seem interested.

One day the librarian was sent a soccer magazine by a friend in the city. For a change she cut out and pinned up some of the best pictures at the far end of the room. Then she wrote on the chalk board in every formroom: 'Who won the World Cup? The answer is in your library.'

It wasn't long before three students were standing at the library door. 'Can we come in wearing our sports clothes?' they asked. The librarian laughed. 'Of course you can, your clothes don't matter. Everyone can use the library!'

The students hurried past the bookshelves and started looking at their heroes in action. They were thrilled by the pictures and told each other so with enthusiasm.

Some girls came to the library door. 'What's all the noise in here?' asked one. The librarian explained that some Form 2 soccer fans were looking at pictures of the World Cup. 'But I thought people had to be quiet in the library, like in church,' said the student. 'Oh no,' replied the librarian, 'you can talk in here if you want, especially if it is about things you find in the library, but try not to shout!'

The girls went over to the posters just as the first group of students had finished. Instead of walking straight out of the library the boys began to look around and see what else they could do. One saw a large map of the country and went to find his village; another began flicking through a copy of Time magazine and one, who hoped to be the school's team captain, began looking for a big book on soccer tips.

That is how students at Riki Oye School found out about the books in their library. Since then the library has been used by students every day, sometimes for study and sometimes just to enjoy looking at pictures of soccer stars!

Figure 1.2 Students reading the sports pages of a newspaper in Beulah Secondary School library

1   What is a school library?

What is a library?

A library is a room or building where books, pamphlets, magazines, newspapers, cassettes and videos are kept together. These items are known as the library's stock. In the stock all kinds of information can be found.

A library may be large or small. Some people think libraries have to be large to work well, but this is not so. Many secondary schools have fewer than 200 books and most primary schools have even fewer. To make the best use of school books you need to organise them carefully, and the best way to do that is by setting up a library.

Why does a school need a library?

A school needs a library because libraries support the school's work of literacy and education.

A school library is useful in literacy work from the earliest stage because it encourages good reading habits to be formed when children are young. All teachers should aim to stimulate children's curiosity about books and to encourage students to start loving the written word. One of the best ways of doing this is to set up a school library with a wide variety of information and fiction books. The vocabulary range of these books should suit all skill levels, so that even reluctant students will be able to read what they want, when they want, for their studies.

A library should also have stock that is fun to read. When students discover that soccer yearbooks, novels and magazines are also in the library they may start to spend some of their leisure time reading. The more students read, the faster their English will improve. This will help them in their studies and when they leave school.

The school library supports the student's studies. Every library collection will have information that can improve students' understanding of the subjects they learn at school, and increase their knowledge of the world. A school library may also have books by local writers that will encourage students' interest and pride in the local area.

As well as providing access to information, a school library allows students to develop the skills of searching for information on their own. This will help to develop a problem-solving and active approach to learning. Pupils who regularly look up information in books will improve both their form work and their reading skills.

Libraries are also very useful for teachers. All staff, whether maths, woodwork, home economics, science or geography teachers, can improve their form teaching by using stock from the library. Libraries are a source of information for every teacher, not just for English teachers. This is especially so if the school library has stock which can:

- give students knowledge (both general knowledge and specific information from set textbooks)
- provide explanations, e.g. about how coal is made or for particular sports rules
- satisfy students' curiosity and interest in life
- offer art, craft, music, dance and cultural information.

Using the books and other stock in the library will help teachers prepare their lessons better. It may also encourage teachers to give students project work that asks them to go to the library and find out information for their form work. This will encourage students to study, learn and achieve better results as well as give them the confidence to start looking for information on their own.

· ·

Teaching tip   *If your students ask why the school needs a library, explain that information can change people's lives for the better. If the world was the size of a village it would be easy to share ideas with all the villagers. But because there are so many people in the world, living far apart and using different languages, the best way of finding new information is through books, pamphlets, magazines and newspapers.*

Imagine, for example, that some agricultural teachers in West Africa have found a way of growing bananas more quickly. How will students and teachers in Pakistan or the Pacific find out about this? One way is by listening to radio programmes such as the BBC World Service's Hello Tomorrow, *but because you hear the information only once it is difficult to remember all the details. If you have a library, however, all you need to do is find the right book or magazine. Then you can read the new information as often as you like.*

Different types of school library

There are three different types of school library. All should be organised so that students and teachers find them easy to use.

Primary school library

In a primary school library it is essential to encourage children to love reading. A good idea is to divide primary school stock into skill levels: books for beginners, and books for children who are just starting to read on their own. Make sure children can easily reach all the stock. You could put books on a low shelf with mats or cushions nearby so that children can look at the books on their own or make themselves very comfortable when their teacher reads them a story.

Secondary school library

In a secondary school library it is important to build on the interest in books and reading developed at primary school. It is essential to provide information books which support students' studies as well as continuing to develop students' reading skills for life.

Formroom library

If your school is unable to find a separate room for the library, or if you have security problems at an existing library, a good way of keeping books safely is to store them in a lockable cupboard. A formroom library may have very few books, but it can be helpful for staff teaching large forms of mixed ability students. See chapter 3 for more about formroom libraries.

2 Preparing to set up your library

· ·

What you need to do first

Before you can open your library, there are ten main tasks that you need to carry out. These are listed below in the recommended order, and are covered in more detail in the following ten chapters.

1   Organise a library committee and decide on library rules, opening times, staffing and the amount of help you need from library monitors.

2   Decide on the method of lending books and how to classify information (non-fiction) books.

3   Prepare the library room, make the bookshelves and organise equipment and stationery.

4   Check that the library is secure.

5   Get to know the different types of library stock and the parts of a book. If you already have a library you may want to remove damaged or inappropriate stock.

6   Make an 'accession register' to record the books that the library receives. Glue the school nameplate and, depending on your lending method, a return date label into all books.

7   Divide books into fiction and information (non-fiction). Divide information books into subject areas according to your chosen method of classification. Give each book a spine label.

8   Make library catalogues. This will include a shelf list and title catalogue.

9   Put books on to shelves. Arrange information books by subject. Arrange fiction books in alphabetical order by the author's last name.

10 Make shelf guides so that books can be found easily and check that your lending system is fully operational. Put up a subject index and posters on the walls to make the library look more attractive and to remind students of any rules about using or borrowing books.

Why you need to do this

It is important to follow a logical order when you set up a library. However time-consuming these tasks seem to be, you will find that careful attention at an early stage will ensure your school has a well organised library. This will encourage students and staff to use the stock and will help you to run the library day by day.

It is important that you share and pass on your library organising skills, so that if you decide to leave the school the library will not close. It often happens that a school has an excellent library for a few years, but then the teacher–librarian leaves and problems start because no one else has the skills to continue running it.

Read the three stories below and decide how you would like your school library to look next month, ten months from now and ten years from now.

The Memory
'That library every day became more like the memory of a library: the shelves lying empty, the piles of books tilting too far over to left or right, missing the intimate touch of their fellow volumes.'
From the Cuban writer G. Cabrera Infante's *Three Trapped Tigers*

The Reality?
'The library was very small and cluttered with formroom sets of books. The stock was minimal and very old . . . Windows leaked so shelving was restricted to the centre of the library . . . Only eight students could use it at one time.'
Donna Wyness, VSO Librarian at Vava'u High School, Tonga, working with Finau Laukau and 'Ana Moimoi

Your Goal
'What a library looks like depends very much on the idea the librarian has of its purpose. If it is just an office where readers can borrow books the library will be a very dull place indeed. If the librarian thinks all it needs are a few shelves of books and a desk for the librarian, no user will spend more time there than is absolutely necessary.'

'If the librarian sees the library as a place where users can study, read or even browse and obtain information of all kinds, or even better: if he or she considers the library to be the social focus of the centre/school then the librarian can make an effort to turn even an unattractive room into an efficient, friendly place where users will be pleased to spend some time and where they feel at home.'
From a library newsletter produced by Ruth Weitzel, working as a VSO librarian in the Caribbean with a number of local colleagues including Laurentia Israel, Jacqueline Mussington, Patricia Baptiste and Nellie Payne

The first library story 'The Memory' is something you should try to avoid. The second story, 'The Reality?', shows the library is badly managed and is hard for students to use: there are no interesting books in it, just textbooks. The third story, 'Your Goal', explains what a good library should be like – friendly, well organised and an enjoyable place for students and teachers to use. Read on to find out how to make your school library a success.

How to start – the library committee

Your first task is to organise a library committee. A library committee will enable you to share library skills and decisions and encourage people to use the library. This is especially important at a secondary school.

How to set up a library committee

One way to set up a library committee which has worked successfully for other school libraries is to include the teacher–librarian as secretary, the head teacher or English teacher as chairperson, and one other teacher. You should also have at least two girl students and two boy students on the committee. There are two ways of choosing students for the library committee: you can either ask students to vote for representatives or you can appoint responsible pupils. The library committee should meet regularly, perhaps once a month or at the start and end of every school term.

As the teacher–librarian you will be an important committee member. To help you advise the committee and suggest ways to improve the library, you should wherever possible arrange a visit to an established library. This could be the national library, an academic library or a specialist library. Ideally you should arrange to work alongside library staff for a few days to familiarise yourself with library routines and procedures. This direct experience of a working library will allow you to visualise the guidelines and alternatives described in this book, and help guide the decisions of the library committee.

What the library committee does

The committee must interpret what users want from their library. The committee will help select books and make management decisions about library opening times, borrowing methods and classification. It will also decide how to spend the budget and perhaps set a caution fee or fine system for books that are returned late and/or are damaged.

A library committee is an excellent way of making your library popular in the school. Because the committee members have helped to make decisions about the project, other staff and students are likely to be encouraged by their enthusiasm.

Here are some comments about library committees from VSO volunteers who have already set up libraries.

'It is best that as many people as possible are involved, then the library is for everybody and any rules are jointly decided . . . You should never attempt to set up a library alone. A more democratic approach is needed. Always invite the principal and heads of departments and always include the learners too! You could also include local donors.'
Marie Bray, Nursing School Library, Nigeria

'If I was setting up a library again I'd try harder to involve staff on a library committee. It's an enormous amount of work running a library so get students involved and make staff take responsibility.'
Nick Hayward, Beulah Secondary School, Solomon Islands

'Members of the library committee included the head teacher, a secondary school inspector, an English teacher and me as secretary. It is now the decision-making, responsible body for the Resource Centre.'
Liz Doyle, Kwale District Resource Centre, Kenya

The library committee also decides which books should be removed from the stock, either because their content is unsuitable or because they are damaged and cannot be repaired. In some countries books are so expensive, and so hard to obtain, that you should be cautious about removing stock just because it is old.

The library committee should agree about which items must stay permanently in the library and should not be lent out. These will include all reference books, and any books the committee wants to look after extra carefully. An example might be *Where There Is No Doctor*. This is a health manual which is very popular because it is well written and makes difficult medical terms easy to understand. If your school library has only one copy of this book, it might be better to keep it in the reference section where students and staff can use it to find quick answers. However, if you have several copies, keep one in the reference section and classify the other copies in the information section so that people can borrow the book if they want.

How to involve other students

Do not let your library committee grow too large: ten people is enough and a smaller number may be even better. However, if there is a lot of interest, make sure students and staff can share their ideas about the library in other ways. This can be done through library monitors, a library club and a suggestions book. Having library monitors and a library club are excellent ideas because students can help you with the day-to-day running of the library at the same time as learning new skills. This will encourage students to keep using libraries when they leave school.

What are library monitors?

Library monitors are responsible students you can train to help with the day-to-day running of the library, for instance issuing books and returning books to shelves. Library monitors can also make new displays, create enthusiasm for competitions and help find 'lost books'.

Becoming a library monitor should be a privilege. You will need about ten students who are really keen to help run the library. One way to choose monitors is to ask students to let you know who wants to be a monitor. If more than ten people are interested, then ask students to vote for their library monitors. It is best to do this by secret ballot, but do try to make sure you have equal numbers of boys and girls chosen as monitors. Alternatively, you could ask form teachers if they would be willing to let students elect one or two people as class monitors. If the forms are mixed sexes, ask for one girl and one boy library monitor from each form.

'There are few women librarians in Bangladesh. It is always noticeable that the users are 95 per cent male.'
Nicole Fitton, Library Adviser in Bangladesh, pointing out the need to try and train more women as librarians

One of the best ways of encouraging more women to become librarians is to get girls to use the library while they are at school. Good ways of involving them are to make them library monitors and to encourage them to join the library club.

What is a library club?

A library club is made up of students interested in learning more about the library and helping with library work. Many schools have clubs that meet once or twice a week for extra woodwork, cooking, sewing, sports or craft lessons. You could use club time to set up a library club. Train library club members to do book repairs and other library duties, such as replacing books on the fiction and information bookshelves. You could ask members to be responsible for making new library displays, pinning up students' work and arranging special trips.

'Organising day trips to places of interest and factories may attract students to join the club. Information about places could be read before trips and then when students return they could write down their experiences.'
Daniel Aidoo, who worked as a library assistant at Central Regional Library, Ghana

What is a suggestions book?
A suggestions book is an exercise book kept in the library which people who are shy, or busy, can use to write down suggestions about the library and titles of books they would like to read. Look at the suggestions book regularly: you are sure to find some ideas in it that will improve your school library.

3   Preparing the library room

What are your library room needs?

Once the library committee has been set up, your next task is to decide where to put the library. There is no such thing as an ideal library room. A library can be big or small, with many books or just a few. The best school library is one that students visit often and where it is easy for users to find the books they want to read.

The library room should be big enough for at least one form of students to visit at the same time. Space limitations may stop you from providing a study area. If this is the case you could put floor cushions or mats in a corner of the room for leisure reading. This is especially good for primary school students and will make the library a popular place for story telling.

Figure 3.1 A school library in Solomon Islands

Windows are essential. They should provide good reading light and ventilation. If the climate is hot, position windows to catch any cross-draft. A hot room makes people want to sleep, not study. In humid countries books may be spoilt by mould if the library room is damp. Good ventilation helps reduce this problem.

Water spoils books, so the library needs a well-maintained roof and overhang. You may like to add a plastic pipe or bamboo gutter to collect any rainwater. Remember to clean the gutter (or put insect netting across it) or students may contract illnesses such as malaria. Shutters also protect stock against heavy rain. If there is any risk of seasonal flooding make sure it is possible to move books to higher shelves quickly.

Libraries can look very different. Figure 3.2 shows one building style that has been used to make a successful school library. A school library should be kept in a separate, lockable room and have well-publicised opening times.

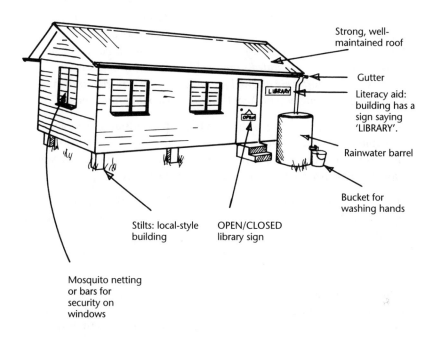

Figure 3.2 A design for a library

How to make your library secure

For most school libraries the biggest problem is security. It is important that your library room is secure. The best way to stop theft is by making it difficult for anyone to take books. Put locks on the door and make sure that windows can be closed with shutters, glass or close-fitting bars. Mosquito netting makes it difficult to pass books out of the window.

If books are kept in a shared formroom, if windows are broken or covered by torn mosquito gauze, of if staff regularly forget to lock doors, books will go missing. Librarians say your library stock will be safer if it is kept in a separate room or building, with only one entrance/exit and with the teacher–librarian's desk placed near the door. It is recommended that you lock your library when staff or library monitors are not in the room.

Your methods of preventing opportunities for people to remove books may not work 100 per cent, as Nick Hayward found when he was teaching English at Beulah Secondary School in Solomon Islands. However, even if security continues to be a problem at your school, make every effort to keep the library open as often as possible and to have well publicised opening times so that students can make the best possible use of the books. Here Nick Hayward describes his experience.

'We tried a variety of strategies including staff involvement, checking students on the way out and leaving bags at the door, but nothing really worked. All this proved very demoralising. However we did achieve things too, the library worked and students read a lot of books! At some schools students were banned from the library because books went missing – only staff were allowed to use the library. I'm glad that even if stock did go missing we still kept the library open and functioning.'

Another way to improve security is to keep essential textbooks in lockable cupboards. If you decide to do this, make sure a list of titles is pinned up where students can easily see it and ensure you have regular times when they can use these books.

'This practice helps protect the stock and students continue to come to the library. If all the important books are lost students will never come to the library.'
Daniel Aidoo, who worked as a library assistant at Central Regional Library in Ghana

Daniel Aidoo also found that theft, and the tearing out of pages, was reduced if students knew photocopies could be organised. This may only be possible for school libraries near a town which has reliable photocopying facilities. If theft is still a problem, you could try the method used by Cynthia Stirrup, whilst working in The Gambia:

'We needed a glass-fronted, lockable bookcase for the most desirable books, such as school textbooks and the **African Writers Series.***'*

This keeps important stock safe and allows students to see which books are available during supervised study times.

It is inevitable that books will be lost and damaged at your school. Staff at big libraries expect about 2 per cent (two out of every 100 books) of their stock to be missing or unusable by the next stocktake. The best approach is to be realistic about theft and damage. Try to prevent damage or theft from happening, but remember when you are thinking about security that the library is meant to be an inviting place for students to study in or visit, so do not make it look like a prison!

A formroom library

If your school does not have a separate room for the library you will have to find another safe place for the books, pamphlets and other stock. This might be the deputy or head teacher's office, a lockable cupboard in a classroom or even some clearly labelled boxes of books that can be kept in a secure place when the teacher–librarian is busy with other duties.

The disadvantages

- The main problem with a formroom library is that students and teachers have limited access. For example, if the room is normally used for teaching, students may only be able to look at or borrow books between lessons. This may make using the library for research difficult and unpopular. It may also encourage people to take books without permission so that they can look at them without time pressures and without lots of other students disturbing them.

- Students may be nervous about entering a teacher's room to choose books.

- Security may still be a problem if the teacher is unwilling to lock up whenever he or she plans to be out of the room, even if it is only for a minute.

'We tried to make the library belong to the students and students' work was displayed. But the library was used for other purposes so there were problems with security and leaving out book displays.'
Donna Wyness, working with Finau Laukau and 'Ana Moimoi, at Vava'u High School, Tonga

The advantage

- A formroom library is a good way of managing books if you are having trouble with security or if you do not have a library room, but your long-term target should be to keep library stock in its own lockable room or building.

What furniture does the library need?

Essential library furniture
- bookshelves
- desks and chair for teacher–librarian.

The basic furnishing equipment for a library is bookshelves. Books last longer and are easier to find if they are displayed on shelves. You can make shelves from many materials: wood, bamboo, bricks and even metal. Before you make or buy shelves remember to think about the height of your students. Shelves at primary schools should not be higher than 120 cm (4 feet). At secondary schools the top of your bookcase should not be higher than 180 cm (6 feet). A 180 cm bookcase with five shelves would hold about 150 books. If your school has no bookshelves and no money, use something else instead – tea chests, for example, or wooden packing cases/boxes. Look at figures 3.3–3.6 for ideas about how to make different types of bookshelves.

'ODA was quite happy for us to import several hundred pounds' worth of book stands, paperback racks, issue trays and library furniture. If the funds had been made directly available all these items could have been made in Zanzibar from local materials by some of Zanzibar's many skilled carpenters.'
Ian Smith, Libraries Adviser, Tanzania

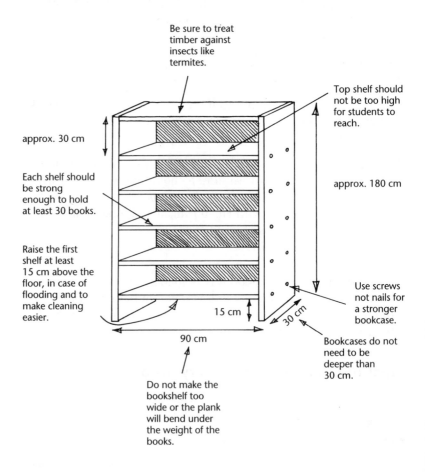

Be sure to treat timber against insects like termites.

Top shelf should not be too high for students to reach.

approx. 30 cm

Each shelf should be strong enough to hold at least 30 books.

approx. 180 cm

Raise the first shelf at least 15 cm above the floor, in case of flooding and to make cleaning easier.

15 cm

30 cm

Use screws not nails for a stronger bookcase.

90 cm

Bookcases do not need to be deeper than 30 cm.

Do not make the bookshelf too wide or the plank will bend under the weight of the books.

Figure 3.3 A wooden five-shelf bookcase

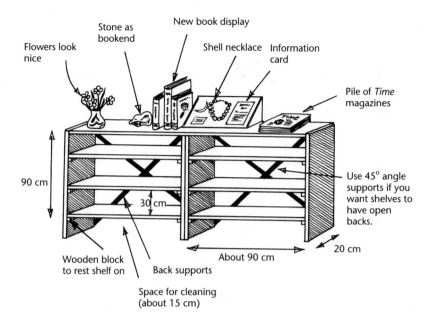

Flowers look nice

Stone as bookend

New book display

Shell necklace

Information card

Pile of *Time* magazines

90 cm

30 cm

Use 45° angle supports if you want shelves to have open backs.

20 cm

Wooden block to rest shelf on

Back supports

About 90 cm

Space for cleaning (about 15 cm)

Figure 3.4 Low wooden shelves with display surface

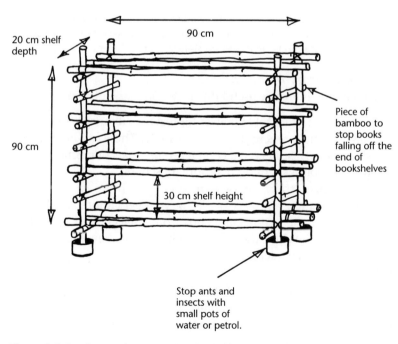

20 cm shelf depth

90 cm

90 cm

Piece of bamboo to stop books falling off the end of bookshelves

30 cm shelf height

Stop ants and insects with small pots of water or petrol.

Figure 3.5 Bamboo or loya cane bookshelves

21

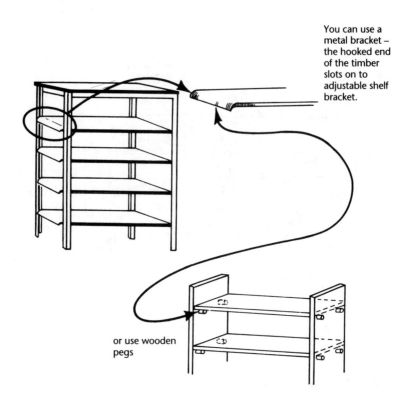

You can use a metal bracket – the hooked end of the timber slots on to adjustable shelf bracket.

or use wooden pegs

Figure 3.6 Adjustable shelves can be made locally. They provide light and airy shelf space which helps to prevent mould. They are very useful if some of your books are too large to put on standard bookshelves.

Optional library furniture
The following items are useful if your school has sufficient funds:

- filing cabinet or lockable drawer for teacher–librarian's use
- desks and chairs where students can study. These can be made of local materials. Students may prefer to use mats or cushions, especially younger children at primary schools
- browser boxes (these are useful boxes in which the teacher–librarian can place books for younger children so they can choose their own reading book from a selection of books at a suitable skill level for their age and ability – see figure 3.7)
- magazine display racks
- display boards fixed to the walls.

'There is no space for desks and chairs so the students made mats to sit on, which many find more comfortable anyway.'
Freda Sanders, Schools Library Adviser, with Julian Treadway, Solomon Islands Teachers' College

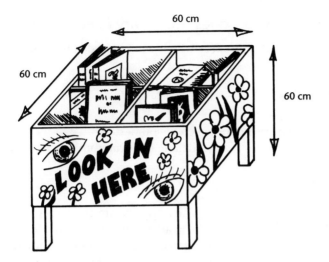

Figure 3.7 A browser box particularly good for primary school children and for sorting odd-sized and large books or magazines.

What equipment does the library need?

In order to run the library efficiently you will need some office equipment. Your school may already own many of these items.

Essential office equipment
- two record or issue boxes, long and narrow to fit record or index cards of a standard 125 x 76 mm (5 x 3 inch) size. You could use a shoebox
- lockable cash box for keeping any petty cash, stamps or library fine money safely
- cleaning utensils: broom, dusters, etc.
- kerosene light (if no electricity) and kerosene. Make sure you store these in a safe place, away from paper and books, to reduce the risk of fire
- rubber stamp of school's name and ink pad
- ruler
- scissors (or knife). These should be kept in a lockable drawer as they can be dangerous
- stapler.

Optional office equipment
- date stamp
- pencil sharpener (you can use a knife but remember to keep this out of reach of younger pupils)
- hole punch
- typewriter
- wastepaper basket.

What stationery does the library need?

Below is a list of stationery which will be needed to help run the library.

Essential stationery
- ballpoint pens
- carbon paper (use this to copy your letters)
- coloured marker pens (indelible ink, waterproof pens are best. Felt pens are acceptable)
- drawing pins
- envelopes
- glue (rubber-based glues, like Copydex, are good, so are glue sticks – buy both if you can). There are many types of glue for sale in shops but some are not suitable for use by young children. Spray glue and extra-strong 'super' glues should be avoided.
- ink pad refills
- masking tape or coloured sticky 'electrical' tape for book repairs and/or classification
- ledger for accession register
- several exercise books, including one for accounts, one for book or magazine orders, one for borrowing records and one for queries and/or suggestions
- paper clips
- pencils
- staples
- sticky tape, dots or labels (plain ones can be coloured with pens if you choose a colour coded classification system). Primary school pupils and their teachers might find it helpful to use colours – for example red, yellow and blue – to divide books into skill levels. This can help young children to select books from the library stock.
- cut and ruled record cards (sometimes called index cards or guide cards). These are sold in packets in a variety of standard sizes. The recommended size is 125 x 76 mm (5 x 3 inches) but as long as they fit the record or issue box it does not matter what size they are. If you find these cards hard to obtain you could make your own. You could also try asking printers for paper offcuts if you have very little money to make library purchases. To make your own record cards cut up stiff paper. Make divider cards of 125 x 85 mm (5 x $3^1/_2$ inches) in the same way, but from coloured card.
- paper.

Optional stationery
- stencils (for making neat posters and shelf guides)
- typewriter ribbon

- Sellotape can be useful, but it tends to dry, shrink and fall off. For small book repairs you could use glue or clear sticky tape like Scotch 3M Magic Tape.

Teaching tips

1 *A bookcase with five shelves of 180 x 90 cm (6 x 3 feet) will hold about 150 books. If your library has this number of books and only one bookcase there may be a problem when students come into the library. They will find it difficult to reach the books on the top shelves and there will be such a crowd that it will be hard for students to find the books they are looking for. In this case it is best to have several lower shelves arranged around the library room, rather than just one bookcase.*

2 *You could ask the woodwork teacher to help you make the library and its furniture. Remind him or her to protect the shelves against warping and insects. If possible, try to make some shelves adjustable (see figure 3.6), so that larger books can be arranged on them too.*

3 *Ask students to make two issue boxes in which you can file the title cards and, depending on your lending method, borrowers' cards. A good alternative is to use clean shoeboxes. Some librarians make a small hole at the bottom of all index cards and then put a thin stick through all the cards to prevent their alphabetical order being accidentally confused. This device saves a lot of time if the issue box is ever dropped.*

How to keep simple accounts

It is essential to keep a record of everything you spend on the library room, furniture, equipment, stationery and stock. This will involve two main tasks.

1 Always ask for a receipt (a note of the cost of your purchases and the date, written on headed paper with the seller's signature) when you buy anything for the library. Keep all receipts in a safe place. At least once a year the school accountant is sure to need to see these receipts.

2 As soon as you have bought any item write down the date, the amount spent and a short description of what you have bought

in your accounts notebook. Your notebook should be ruled into four columns headed **Date, What bought?, Price** and **Total**.

Why keep accounts?

Keeping account records helps you check how much money you have spent on the library. It will also help you budget how much money you need to spend on the library next year. The school accountant will also need to see your records.

4 Getting to know your library stock

What stock is in your library?

When you organise your library, it is important to get to know the range and type of stock you have and to divide your stock into three basic sections – reference, information and fiction.

Reference material

This includes encyclopaedias, dictionaries and atlases. Reference books are used to find quick answers, check facts, answer students' questions and discover new information. Because reference books are often large, expensive and in constant demand, most libraries do not lend them. Instead librarians put them on clearly labelled reference bookshelves next to the information books.

Information material

This is sometimes known as non-fiction and is stock about people, places and things. Most of the stock in your library, including textbooks, will belong to this group. To help library users find the book they want, it is recommended that the teacher–librarian organises all the information stock into different subject areas. For example, put all the books on trees and forests on bookshelves close to each other. You will read more about how to do this in chapter 7.

Fiction

These books are also known as story books or novels. Some fiction books are used by English teachers in secondary schools all round the world; *Animal Farm* by George Orwell and *Things Fall Apart* by Chinua Achebe are two examples. Fiction books are not just for studying, they can also be read for fun: *Tales Of The Tikongs* by Epeli Hau'opa is a good example of a novel that students will enjoy.

Once you have divided the stock into reference, information and fiction sections, it will be clear to you that the stock comes in many different shapes and forms – including books, pamphlets, booklets, magazines, newspapers, flipcharts, posters, photo albums of school forms, maps, videos, audio cassettes, etc. The most important type of stock, however, will be the books.

More about books

Books are made of paper and so they can be easily damaged. It is just as important to show students how to treat books well as it is to encourage them to make more use of the books in the library. One way to do both is to make sure that students and library monitors know all about what a book is and are able to name the different parts of a book.

How to help students learn about the parts of a book

The best method is to give a form lesson. Give each student a book. Then point out the different parts of a book and explain their purpose. Ask students to find the same parts on their own book. Remember to explain the uses of the contents and index pages as these can help students with their studies. Use figures 4.1 and 4.2 and the information below. For more ideas about library lessons see chapters 13 and 14.

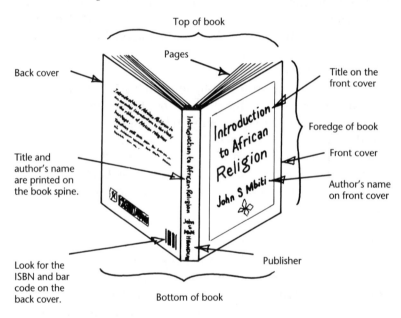

Figure 4.1 Learning about the parts of a book

The parts of a book

- **Cover**   This can be hard (hardback) or soft (paperback). The cover helps protect the book. Some teacher–librarians like to put an extra cover, which they buy from library suppliers or make from strong paper or sticky-back plastic, on popular books.

- **Front cover**   This may have a picture on it and usually has the title of the book and the author's name; it may also have the publisher's name.

- **Back cover**   This often has a summary of what the book is about; or it may have some people's comments about how much they enjoyed the book – these are called reviews. Most back covers list the book's own internationally recognised ten-digit ISBN, usually nowadays in the form of a computer readable bar code. An ISBN is a computer number used by publishers and booksellers to identify a title. In some large bookshops you will be able to order the books you want if you give the bookseller just this number. However, it is not essential information for libraries without computers.

- **Spine**   This is the backbone of a book. If it breaks, or is damaged, there is a risk that the book's pages will fall out. On the spine most books usually have the title of the book and the author as well as a symbol (picture or letters) which identifies the publisher.

- **Spine label**   All the books in your library should have a spine label, glued or stuck to the bottom of the spine. This will be used by students to locate books they want and to find out if the book is information or fiction; it will also give a visual reminder of what the book is about. If, for example, a student is looking for a biology book, he or she (depending on your classification system) would look for green spine labels or the classification code number 500. (See chapter 7 for more information about classification systems.)

- **Title page**   This is usually a right-hand page near the front of the book. On it will be the book's title, author and publisher.

- **Title verso page**   This is traditionally the left-hand page immediately after the title page. On it will be more information about the publisher (for example, the publisher's address) and about the book (what year it was published, if it has been reprinted and who printed it). The title verso page will also have details of the book's copyright.

- **School nameplate and return date label**   It is recommended that you glue your school nameplate and a return date label on to the first right-hand page as you open the book (see figure 4.3). Explain to students that this shows who owns the book and that it is also the place to find out what day they should return the book if they have borrowed it from the library.

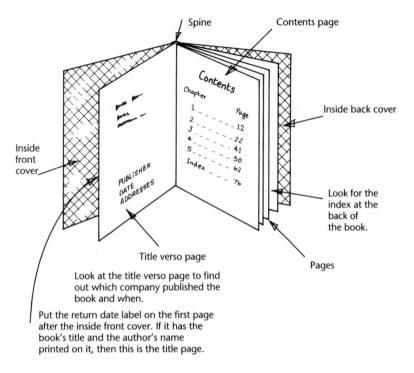

Spine

Contents page

Inside back cover

Inside front cover

Inside back cover

Look for the index at the back of the book.

Title verso page

Pages

Look at the title verso page to find out which company published the book and when.

Put the return date label on the first page after the inside front cover. If it has the book's title and the author's name printed on it, then this is the title page.

Figure 4.2 Learning about the inside of a book

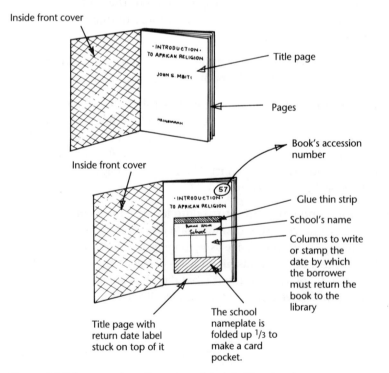

Inside front cover

Title page

Pages

Inside front cover

Book's accession number

Glue thin strip

School's name

Columns to write or stamp the date by which the borrower must return the book to the library

Title page with return date label stuck on top of it

The school nameplate is folded up $1/3$ to make a card pocket.

Figure 4.3 Where to place the return date label in a book

- **Contents page**   Most information books have a contents page. This gives an outline, or sometimes a brief summary, of what will be in each chapter – and a page number so that you can turn straight to the right chapter. For example, in a book on the lifecycle of a butterfly you might see from the contents page that chapter 1 is on larvae, chapter 2 is on the chrysalis, chapter 3 is on caterpillars and chapter 4 is on butterflies. If you want more detailed information then you should look at both the contents page and the index.

- **Index**   An information book is more useful if it has an index. This is usually an alphabetical list of subjects, people and other important items that are written about in the book, each with a page reference. An index is usually at the back of a book. The page references make it easy for the user to find the information they want. For example, use the index in this book to find out where there is more information about different types of stock. After the word 'stock', you will find several numbers. These numbers direct you to the pages in the book which have information about stock printed on them. Make sure your students do not confuse an index with a glossary (or key words section), which lists difficult or foreign words and explains what they mean, but does not give page references.

Before students use the library, check that they know what is the front cover, the back cover and the spine; how to tell the title from the author (this can be quite difficult for students); who the publisher is; where to find the publication date and where to find your own library details, like the return date label.

· ·

***Teaching
tip***   *Your students may be set a project that asks them one question about how to grow rice, one question on how to make aeroplanes and one question on Nelson Mandela's work in South Africa.*

Explain that if they want quick answers to these questions they need to find a reference book and use the index. In the index they should look for the best possible word that describes the subject they want – (in this case the words would be 'rice' 'aeroplanes' and 'Mandela').

If they want more detailed information they should go to the appropriate bookshelf in the library, and then check the contents and index pages of relevant books.

· ·

How to help students keep books in good condition

It is unfair to blame students for spoiling books if they have not been taught how to look after them. It can be tempting to tell students not to write inside a book; not to have dirty hands; not to take books out in the rain; not to bend the corners of the page when they forget their bookmarks; not to eat in the library; not to pull the book's spine when they are taking a book off a shelf . . . but lists of 'Don't do this' and 'Don't do that' can discourage students from using books. Instead explain to students that because books are expensive, and can be easily damaged, they must be treated with respect.

Simon Etherton trained 12 student library monitors including Stephen Kapu and Nester Haiptu to help run the library at Allardyce Secondary School, Solomon Islands. He suggests:

'There is a lack of understanding about how fragile books are. Students need constant reminding about how to turn over pages and why they should use paper bookmarks (rather than pens, rulers or even other books).'

Using a library and its books requires skills. All school children will need patient, repeated explanations and a good example set by the teacher–librarian and other staff. Remember also to make the library a friendly place, otherwise students will not use it.

More about other types of stock

Most libraries have a variety of stock besides books. This may include magazines, newspapers, pamphlets and audio-visual stock. The rest of this chapter looks at different types of stock that might be good for your school library.

Newspapers

Newspapers can be published daily or weekly. They are often very popular with students at school libraries, especially if they are local publications containing up-to-date news. However, old newspapers soon turn yellow and attract dirt, insects and mice. A good idea is to save back copies and then when you have a year's collection, to arrange for them to be bound inside a strong hard-backed cover. Daniel Aidoo, working as a library assistant at Central Regional Library in Ghana, found:

'Bound volumes of periodicals [magazines] and newspapers are very popular with students and are also helpful for reference purposes.'

If you decide to bind your newspapers it is recommended that you let students read the issues for one or two weeks before you remove them from the library. Then you can store the newspapers in a dry place, in a pile arranged in date order, ready for binding at the end of the year.

An alternative is to remove newspapers from the library after three months, and then to cut out the most interesting stories and organise them into general sections in a subject file or project box (see p. 36). In this way you could create subject files on, for example, the Life of Ghandi; Leatherback turtles; the Aswan Dam; etc.

Another alternative is to do what Ruth Weitzel, working in the Caribbean with librarians including Laurentia Israel, Jacqueline Mussington, Patricia Baptiste and Nellie Payne, suggests:

'Rather than throw away unwanted issues of newspapers and magazines, put them on a free table at the entrance to be given away. Some students might appreciate the materials.'

Magazines

Magazines are publications produced on a regular basis, for instance quarterly, monthly or weekly. They are often in colour and have news items, feature stories, photos and advertisements inside. A magazine can be on any subject: world events, soccer, fashion, business, etc. Famous world-circulation magazines include *Time* and *Newsweek* (both report international events each week); *National Geographic* (which has excellent photographs of people and the world); *New Scientist* (about science); *The Economist* (a business magazine) and *New Internationalist* (facts about people's lives around the world, and particularly developing countries).

The best magazines for secondary schools have plenty of pictures that will raise students' curiosity. A carefully chosen display of magazine pictures and picture captions on the wall can make reluctant readers more enthusiastic about reading short news items.

Both magazines and newspapers can be displayed in browser boxes or on special magazine racks. If you do not have these you could make tidy piles of magazines so that students know where to find their favourite newspapers or magazine. Each magazine should have its own pile, with issues placed in date order – the newest on top.

You can also bind magazines – see the section on newspapers. Figure 12.3 in chapter 12 shows how to make a strong magazine folder.

Pamphlets

Pamphlets are small, thin books which contain information about one subject. They are sometimes called booklets. They look different from other books because they do not have a spine. This means that if you arrange them on the bookshelves you cannot read the title or the name of the author. One way to store pamphlets is to put them in a project box. Because pamphlets are cheaper (and quicker) to make than books, they often contain useful, up-to-date information – for example health and nutrition advice or advice about how to run a business.

Figure 4.4 shows the differences between a book, a pamphlet and a magazine.

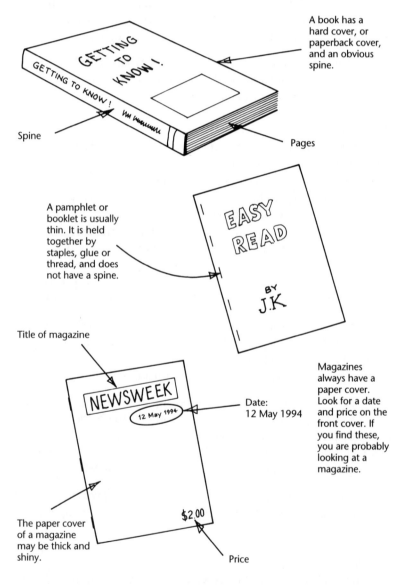

A book has a hard cover, or paperback cover, and an obvious spine.

Spine

Pages

A pamphlet or booklet is usually thin. It is held together by staples, glue or thread, and does not have a spine.

Title of magazine

Magazines always have a paper cover. Look for a date and price on the front cover. If you find these, you are probably looking at a magazine.

Date:
12 May 1994

The paper cover of a magazine may be thick and shiny.

Price

Figure 4.4 Differences between a book, a pamphlet and a magazine

Flipcharts

Flipcharts are like teachers' form notes but they are drawn on several pieces of poster-size paper. Flipcharts can save teachers a lot of time, as they are a permanent record of diagrams that take several minutes to draw on the chalkboard, only to be wiped out by the next teacher.

Encourage teachers to make flipcharts (e.g., of the life cycle of a frog for biology, or on how to vote in an election) for the subjects they teach and then store them safely in the library. The best method is to roll the flipcharts up, and label them clearly on the outside. Make a cross-reference in the shelf guide and catalogue if you have one. Then store the flipcharts in a project box, away from dust.

Maps and posters

The best place for all maps and posters is pinned up on the library walls or on formroom walls. Libraries look more interesting if you display lots of colourful posters. If you are unable to display all your posters, store them in a dust-free area – either folded in project boxes, rolled up in cardboard poster tubes or in a cupboard.

Video cassettes, film reels and music tapes

These are all audio-visual or audio equipment. They are usually supplied in their own cases or boxes to protect them from dust. If your school is in a humid climatic zone add a small packet of silica gel to protect them. This works like a sponge absorbing the moisture in the air. Silica gel is blue but as it absorbs moisture it turns pinky purple, and then pink. Once it is pink it stops absorbing moisture. You do not have to throw out silica gel when you have used it. Just heat it up (over a low temperature) so that it dries out and turns blue again, ready to be re-used. Silica gel can be bought from chemists or pharmacy stores. If you have never seen it before, ask people who are keen photographers to explain more about how it works.

Audio-visual stock will include films and videos; audio stock will include cassettes of music, oral (spoken) history and stories. Both audio-visual and audio stock are useful because they allow students to see things and hear sounds they may find hard to imagine. Used well they can be excellent teaching tools. The problem is that you will need electricity, or a generator, or batteries to use them. They must also be stored carefully. If you have not yet used audio-visual material for teaching purposes, and feel nervous about using it, don't worry. Just experiment – the results are usually very good. Morgan Armstrong, working at Pawa, an isolated, rural secondary school in Solomon Islands, found that:

'Every reading passage and book has to be selected carefully when new words, ideas and concepts are introduced because students want to know: "What's a car, a light bulb or a crime?"'

What would be a good way of showing students this information? Take the example of a car. You could describe a car, draw a car on a chalkboard or pass a picture of a car around the form. But a better way might be to use audio-visual equipment to show a film about cars: *Chitty Chitty Bang Bang* and *Grease* are two good examples. It is often possible to borrow films on educational topics. Many schools like to arrange at least one film or video night a term, and even if they do not have electricity they are often able to hire a generator. Social nights like this are often an excellent way of helping students learn more about the world.

Project boxes and subject files

Project boxes and subject files are two very similar ways of storing stock such as newspaper articles, magazine cuttings, postcards or pictures, all dealing with the same interesting subject. They are very useful places for collecting information about your country or local activities, especially if there are not many books on these subjects in your library. Give your project boxes a title so that you can file them in the title catalogue.

A project box is usually made of wood or plastic or strong card (like a cereal packet, for example). You can store odd-shaped stock such as thin pamphlets, maps and video tapes in them.

Subject files are sometimes called clip files. To make a subject file use an A4 ringbinder file. Decide what information you plan to collect and write a suitable title on the file's spine (e.g., Malaria, Government elections, Reggae music or Cocoa prices). Then cut out each article carefully and glue it on to a piece of A4 paper, remembering to write the name of the publication where you took it from, and the date, on the paper. A good place for this information is the top right-hand corner of the page. Build up subject files for your school with the help of library club members or library monitors.

5 Choosing stock for the library

What stock does the library need?

A school library needs a variety of books that will be useful for students and teachers. This should include:

- some textbooks for form work. You should aim for multiple copies so that students share with as few other students as possible
- reference books that provide quick answers, for example an encyclopaedia, a dictionary, a thesaurus and an atlas
- information (non-fiction) books that students can borrow
- fiction books that students can borrow.

If your school library has been open for some time it may already have a variety of books and other stock. You need to look at every item of stock and decide if it is suitable for the library. Books that are not suitable should be removed.

What makes an information book suitable for the library?

To answer this question you will need to look carefully at the books and other library materials the school owns. As a rule, reference and information books should:

- give students knowledge (both general knowledge and specific information from set textbooks)
- provide explanations (e.g., how coal is made)
- satisfy students' curiosity and interest in life
- offer art, craft, music, dance and cultural information.

Use the seven questions below to find out if your reference and information books are useful for the school library. It is important to involve other teachers when assessing or selecting books. Ask their advice about books in the subjects they teach. Score one point for a 'yes' answer to each question.

1   Is a book on this **subject** needed by students and teachers at the school?

2   Is the book **accurate**? This can be hard to judge, so ask other teachers what they think.

3   Is the author giving two sides of the story? Does it have **balance**?

4   Is the book **up to date**? This is important because information changes quickly, especially in medicine and science. Old atlases may have maps of countries in them that do not exist now! Look up the name of a country that you know has changed and check if the book is correct.

5   Will students find the book **easy to read**? Is it of an **appropriate reading level**? At primary schools books should be as attractive as possible. Young children find too many words on a page dull, but colour pictures will interest them. At secondary schools the best information books use a print that is easy to read. They are written in easily understood English, using simple words and short sentences. The text is made clearer by pictures, photos, diagrams, cartoons and maps. Older books often have no colour pictures and this can make them seem boring for students.

6   Is there a **contents page** and an **index**?

7   Is the book in **good condition**? If it is old or the pages are torn ask yourself if it can be mended. If you cannot repair the book it is not suitable for the library.

Useful books will score full marks, i.e. seven. Books with a very low score should be removed from the library.

Figure 5.1 Teachers at Migwani Teachers' Resource Centre, Kenya, discussing books and assessing their suitability

What makes a fiction book suitable for the library?
A fiction book is suitable if it is enjoyable to read, written at a level that students can understand and does not include material that is sexist, racist or otherwise vetoed by the library committee.

Fiction books may sometimes be used for study, but they should also be read for fun by both students and staff during leisure time. You should aim to have a wide variety of fiction books with vocabulary that suits all skill levels. Practice will help you recognise a good fiction book but this is easier to do if you read the books yourself.

Why remove some books from the library?

Your aim should be to have a collection of well-used, informative and enjoyable books in the library. It is better to have a small stock of interesting books than a large collection that nobody reads. To achieve this you must sort through your existing stock carefully and remove books that are of no value to a school library.

How do you decide which books to remove?

Experienced librarians have found the following to be true.

- Older books may contain out-of-date ideas.

- Books that are sexist and/or racist are not appropriate for libraries.

- Books using old-fashioned words may be hard for students to understand.

- Books that look boring or are falling apart will not be read.

- Unused books attract insects.

Look at all gift books extra carefully. Donated books may not be what you want, or what the students need. Here are comments from two VSO teacher–librarians. They demonstrate the importance of looking carefully at all stock and deciding if it will be suitable for the students.

'The lower level language books, often donations, are inappropriate for the age of the students. Because they do not stimulate their interest, they do not stimulate students' desire to read.'
Donna Wyness, working at Vava'u High School in Tonga with Finau Laukau and 'Ana Moimoi

*'Be wary of free book offers. They are usually unsuitable. However, in cases of very limited funds it is sometimes worth investigating all sources of books. However useless they may seem, it's actually possible to extract a few good titles. And students' taste cannot always be predicted. For example, one volunteer in her school found that one of the most popular titles in the library was **Practical Beekeeping** even though none of her students kept bees.'*
Chris Lane, Kenya

It is also important to be careful about the subject matter. In some countries books about politics, sex education, pregnancy and sicknesses like AIDS may be culturally inappropriate. If you have any doubts, check with your head teacher. The head may ask you to cut out some of the pictures or even pages. Remember that although there may be taboo subjects, people will be curious about all sorts of things. Simon Etherton, working at Allardyce Secondary School in the Solomon Islands, with student librarians Stephen Kapu and Nester Haiptu, says:

'Students are desperate for information, especially on the AIDS disease – and soccer.'

Deciding which books should be removed can be difficult. You may find it helpful to make these decisions with the library committee. Together you will need to decide which books are to be thrown out, which sold and which given away. You could also try contacting the librarian at the nearest local library for advice. Other librarians and teacher–librarians may have faced similar decisions and be able to give a great deal of support if there are strong feelings about, for example, allowing a teenager to read a sex education book or removing particular items of old stock.

If the library committee decides some books are not suitable for the library, they could be sold to raise funds to buy books that are needed. Or you could give away old magazines to students and their families. This is especially useful if you have a large collection of old magazines, and no plans to bind them into sets.

• •

Teaching tip *If your school already has a library collection with an accession register, it is important to cross off each item in the accession register, shelf list and title catalogue, as you remove if from the library. If you forget to do this you will find it hard to stocktake and may think books have been stolen.*

• •

What else is useful for a library?

Most libraries have more books than any other type of stock. But newspapers, maps, flipcharts, pamphlets, posters, audio-visual equipment, books in the home languages of the students, books written by local writers, postcards of well-known national and international scenes, photocopies of interesting articles and journals are all useful for a library. When you are choosing stock for your library, remember to consider all these different types of stock. But only add to your library items which you *know* will be useful for students and teachers.

A good idea for building up a section about local life is to encourage students to make their own books. Add the best ones to the library's stock.

Encourage students to make suggestions about books they would like in the school library. Even if you are sure you know what students should be reading, it is more interesting for the students to read a book they have chosen themselves, than to be given a book and told to read it.

6 Making an accession register

··

When you have weeded through and familiarised yourself with existing stock, or if you are setting up a completely new library and have chosen and received a supply of new books, the next task is making an accession register.

What is an accession register?

An accession register is a record of items of stock in the library in the order in which the library receives them. Every item of stock should be given a unique number when it arrives at the school. This number must be written down both in the accession register and on the item of stock. It is essential that you give all books an accession number and enter them into the accession register.

Why have an accession register?

The accession register shows the teacher–librarian what stock is owned by the school. This is particularly important if the school has several books with the same title, for example, textbooks for form lessons. Because every book is given a unique accession number it will always be possible to identify a particular book.

'This means a borrower cannot say they have returned the book just because another book, with the same title, is on the shelf.'
Cynthia Stirrup who worked in The Gambia

The accession register therefore makes stocktaking easier.

How do you make an accession register?

The detailed instructions below explain how to make and maintain an accession register.

1   Find a large, strong exercise book. (A hardback book would be best – some stationery shops call them ledgers.)

2   Write 'Accession Register' on the front cover.

3   Study figure 6.1. Then rule up four columns in your accession register, as shown in the first part of figure 6.1.

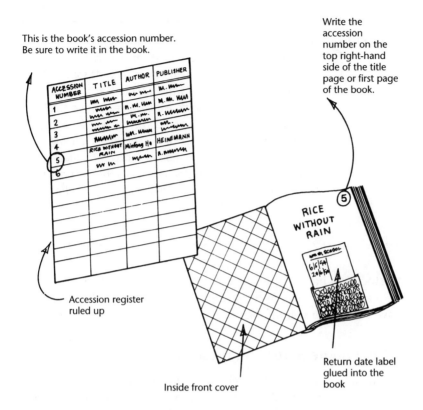

This is the book's accession number. Be sure to write it in the book.

Write the accession number on the top right-hand side of the title page or first page of the book.

Accession register ruled up

Inside front cover

Return date label glued into the book

Figure 6.1 Making an entry in an accession register

4　Take any library book. This will be number 1 in your accession register. Write down the book's title, author and publisher in the columns beside the accession number. Keep the details brief as other information, such as the publication date, ISBN and number of pages, can be entered on the title catalogue cards and shelf list cards. (You will learn about these in chapter 8.)

5　Write the book's accession number inside the book. A good place to write this number is on the top right-hand side of the first page. It is best to write all accession numbers in the same place in every book. For some items, such as audio-visual stock, you may need to use a marker pen to write the accession number on the tape or reel.

6　Take another library book. This will have accession number 2. Follow steps 4 and 5 as above.

7　Give each item in your library stock a different accession number. This is especially important if there are several copies of the same book, as is likely to be the case with textbooks.

8　If you remove any stock from your library, remember to cross out the entry in the accession register.

Teaching *If younger students are helping you make an accession*
tip *register you may need to help them identify the*
difference between a title and an author. At some schools
the teacher–librarian will write a list of books, underlining
the title and author in different colours. You may feel
that underlining the title and author's name in different
colours seems to take a great deal of time but it will
ensure that the accession register is accurate, that
students begin to understand the different parts of the
book and that students are involved in making the
library right from the start.

All stock will have a title, but some will not have an author. If you
are making an accession register entry for a book like this, just
leave the author column blank.

School nameplates and return date labels

When all your books have their own accession number you will
need to glue the school's nameplate and a return date label on to
the first page (or alternatively the back page) of the book. It is
important that all books are seen to belong to the school library.
When you make nameplates it is useful to include the school's
address. If you have a rubber stamp of the school's name you
should also stamp the book in two places – once on the inside back
cover of the book and once on a page in the middle of the book.
This means that if the book is lost it has a better chance of being
returned to the school library.

Which books need a return date label?

All books which the library is going to lend need a return date
label. This tells the borrower when the book is due to be returned.
Reference books, such as dictionaries, encyclopaedias and atlases,
are not usually lent by the library and therefore do not need a
return date label. They do, however, need a school nameplate and
address glued on to one of the first pages.

Before you give a book a return date label you must decide what
method of lending books you plan to have at your school library.
(The various methods are described in chapter 11.)

If you plan to lend books using the exercise book method or the
borrower cards method (see chapter 11), all stock will need a place

where you can stamp the date it should be returned. It is recommended that you do this by making a combined school nameplate and return date label as described below, but you will not need to make your nameplate with a card pocket.

If you plan to lend books using the book ticket system (again, see chapter 11), you must make a joint school nameplate and return date label with a pocket as described below.

How do you make a school nameplate and return date label with a pocket?

Nameplates and return date labels with a pocket can be made by taking a half sheet of A4 paper and folding up approximately one-third, as shown in figure 6.2. Glue down the pocket edges and then glue the top edge of the return date label into the book. At the top of your return date label write, or stamp, the school's name and address.

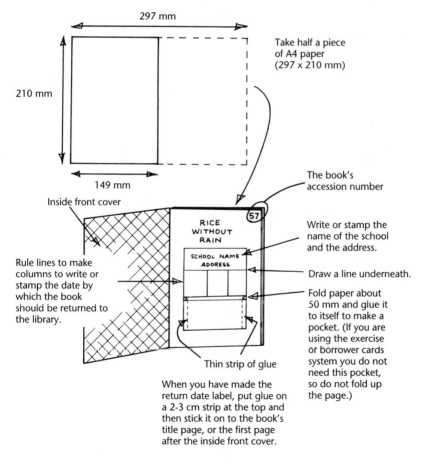

Figure 6.2 How to make a school nameplate and return date label

If you have access to a stencil this might save you time, as Christine George, working in Sierra Leone, found:

'Return date labels can also be made by typing a stencil, which takes about nine labels, and have them run off on duplicating paper.'

• •

Teaching tip   *It is important to process new books as soon as you can. If your school library is sent a large number of books at the same time, it may be useful to keep two or three of them off the shelves in order to show the next group of student library monitors or club members exactly how to add a book to the accession register and where to glue in the return date label.*

• •

The next task is to separate your fiction books from the other books. The library's information books can then be divided into subjects. This task, known as classification, is explained in the next chapter.

7 Organising your books – classification

Your books should now be divided into reference, information and fiction books, and every book should have been entered into the accession register. The next step is to classify the information books.

What is classification?

Classification is a method of organising book titles, so that books on the same subject are kept near each other on the bookshelf.

To organise information books (also called non-fiction books) the best method is to divide your school's stock into different subject areas and then give each book a classification label using a code. You can code by letter, number or colour.

Why do information books need to be classified?

Classification is essential because it keeps information books on the same subject together. This means students and teachers can find the information they want as quickly as possible. Once they understand the library classification system they will know where to find the books they are looking for.

What stock is not classified?

Fiction books are not classified into subject sections; they are filed alphabetically instead. Read more about this in chapter 9. General information books, such as encyclopaedias, should be put into the reference section. Reference books should not be lent by the library. Large books that do not fit on to the book shelves *are* classified into the relevant subject area, but they are shelved in special bookcases for oversize books.

How do you decide which subject area each book belongs in?

Three alternative classification systems are explained in this chapter. They are suitable for different library situations. Whichever system you choose, you will have to decide upon the main subject of each book. Sometimes this can be difficult and people may not agree on the main subject.

What is a subject?

A subject is an area of knowledge. Major library subjects might include agriculture, health, religion and sport. Imagine a row of boxes with subject titles (e.g. Health, Agriculture) printed on the outside of each box. Inside the boxes will be stories and information about different aspects of a particular subject. In the Health box, for example, will be material on first-aid, inoculations, barefoot doctors, hospitals, etc.

Task

Look at the list below. Decide which are main subjects that should go on the outside of the boxes and which are types of information that should go inside the boxes.

- Agriculture
- Bee keeping
- Religion
- The Bible
- Technology
- Second World War aeroplanes

Answer

The main subjects are agriculture (bee keeping is a type of agriculture); religion (the Bible belongs in this subject box) and technology (material on Second World War aeroplanes belongs in this box).

You may find that some books seem to fit into several subjects. Take, for example, an imaginary book called *Economic Miracle: Rice growing in the Philippines*. Would you put this book in the business section (economics); the religion section (miracle); the agriculture section (rice) or the geography section (Philippines)? Of course the book does not actually exist, but if it did I think I would put it in the business section, because it seems to be about economics. What do you think?

How do you choose the best classification method for your school library?

There is a choice for you to make now. You need to decide which of the following classification systems best meets the needs of the students and teachers running and using the library. It is important to remember that whatever classification system you choose you will then need to follow the same book labelling procedure, as explained at the end of this chapter.

Timetable classification

This is the method recommended for primary school libraries.

List all the subjects on the timetable at your school. Your list will probably look similar to this: mathematics, English, science, agriculture, woodwork, home economics, business, sport, religious education, history, geography, music, technology, general knowledge.

Now think about the books you entered into the accession register. Are they books that fit into these subject areas? If the answer is 'yes', you could use these subjects as the basis of classification in your library. If not, you can adjust the subject as required. You could then divide the books into subjects and give them the simple classification codes shown in the table below. For instance, an arithmetic book would be classified under the timetable subject mathematics and given the classification code MATHS on its spine label. (See the section 'How to make spine labels' on p. 55.)

Because some books and pamphlets have very narrow spines, and because some subjects have long names, even neat writing may be hard to fit on to the label. This is why the shorthand codes for each subject, like GEOG for geography, are used for the spine labels instead of the full subject name.

Timetable classification

Timetable subject	Quick label code
Reference	REF
Religions	REL
English grammar	ENG
Science	SCI
Technology and woodwork	TEC
Environment	ENVIRO
Business	BUS
Agriculture	AGRIC
Art	ART
Sport	SPORT
Music	MUS
Home economics	HOME
History	HIST
Geography	GEOG
Mathematics	MATHS

Dewey Decimal Classification (DDC)

The Dewey Decimal Classification is used throughout the world and is popular with many libraries. It is most useful for secondary school libraries with more than 500 information books.

At its simplest, the Dewey system classifies books into ten broad subject areas, which are coded by numbers. Each book has a spine label with a number shown on it, and that number tells the reader what subject area the book belongs in. Particular subject areas are given a range of code numbers recognised throughout the world. The ten ranges start with the numbers 000, 100, 200, 300, 400, 500, 600, 700, 800, 900. So, for example, if you want to classify a science book, you will look at the Dewey Decimal Classification schedule and see that science books take the code classification number 500 or 500-and-something (i.e. the range of numbers from 500 to 599). The science section will include books on a wide-range of sciences, e.g. chemistry, physics, biology and maths.

Dewey Decimal Classification

Standard subject	Code number
Reference	000
Philosophy	100
Religions	200
Social sciences	300
Languages	400
Science	500
Technology	600
Arts and recreation	700
Literature	800
History and geography	900

Each of the ten Dewey subject areas can be sub-divided into more specific areas. For example, in the science section (Dewey number 500) there are ten main subdivisions: 500, 510, 520, 530, 540, 550, 560, 570, 580 and 590.

Dewey Decimal Classification – Science section

500 – Science	Dewey number
General science	500
Mathematics	510

Astronomy	520
Physics	530
Chemistry	540
Geology	550
Fossils	560
Biology	570
Botany	580
Animals	590

If you wanted to look for information about trees, you would go to the nearest related subject area, which would be botany (580). Using the DDC schedule you would find that information about trees is classified at 582.

If you are hoping to add more books to your library, perhaps aiming at a stock of more than 500 information books, the Dewey Decimal system can be very useful. This is because it works on a standard decimal system so that however much new knowledge is discovered or whatever is invented, a place can be made for new subjects in the classification.

Look again at the table on science (500). Within the ten broad subject divisions more subject areas can be made. In the Dewey system the decimal point is used so information can be even further subdivided. This is done by adding figures before or after a decimal point in the closest related classification section. For example, you can find information on geology at 551. Information books about the weather are classified as a subdivision of geology and meteorology, but because the weather is a large subject the decimal point is used. This means that all information books on the climate, clouds, snow and wind, etc., will be classified under the Dewey system at 551.6.

Here is another example: if your library obtained a set of books on local poetry the books would be classified under literature. The existing subjects under literature (800) might be poems (821) and drama/plays (822). Using the Dewey system the new local poetry books could be given the classification number 821.8 for local poetry collections. They would then be placed on the shelves next to the general poetry books, but before the drama books.

It is not essential to use the Dewey method in your library, but if you do decide to use it, the science shelves (Dewey Decimal Classification number 500) might look like this:

Dewey Decimal Classification – science shelves

Standard subject	Dewey number
Science	500
Maths	510
Algebra	512
Geometry	516
Physics	530
Mechanics	531
Heat	536
Chemistry	540
Geology	550
Climate and weather	551.6
Rocks	552
Biology	570
Seasons	574.2
Ecology	574.5
Fish	597
Birds	598
Mammals	599

What are the problems with Dewey Decimal Classification?

Your library books should fit into the ten general subject areas, but even at secondary schools you will probably find that certain sections, e.g. philosophy (100), have no stock. For this reason not all librarians think Dewey is the best classification system for schools. If you only have a few books the shelves can look rather odd, with unclear subject links between neighbouring books.

Some teacher–librarians also say that students find Dewey hard to understand. You must think about students' needs and how easy it will be for them to find the information they want. In general Dewey is a useful classification system, but you might find it appropriate to adapt it slightly.

One adaptation is to use a simple classification code number to show students what subject a book covers. Instead of writing 200 for religion and making subdivisions within this – e.g. 210, 220, etc. for different subdivisions within religion – it is acceptable to code all books on the subject of religion with a 2, losing the noughts and further subdivision numbers.

The simplified code would look like this:

Simplified Dewey Decimal Classification

Standard subject	Simple code
Reference	0 (instead of 000)
Philosophy	1 (instead of 100)
Religions	2 (instead of 200)
Social sciences	3 (instead of 300)
Languages	4 (instead of 400)
Science	5 (instead of 500)
Technology	6 (instead of 600)
Arts and recreation	7 (instead of 700)
Literature	8 (instead of 800)
History and geography	9 (instead of 900)

This is a useful adaptation as it keeps your library collection classified in broad Dewey divisions, but is easy for students to understand quickly.

Classification by Junior Colour Code

Another very good adaptation of the Dewey system is known as the Junior Colour Code. It is recommended that you use this classification system in a secondary school library with fewer than 500 information books.

The advantage of Junior Colour Code classification is that books are divided into the same subject areas as the Dewey system. However, each subject area is given a Dewey code number *and* a special colour. Many students find it easier to look for coloured labels on books than to look for a classification number. If, in the future, the teacher–librarian receives a large collection of information books, changing the library classification system to Dewey will be simple. All you will need to do is to stop adding coloured labels to the spines of the books.

With the Junior Colour Code system the user can recognise the information book they want by the colour on the spine label of the book as well as by the number. For example, an information book about growing maize would be given a red coloured spine label and the Dewey classification number 600, and would be put on the bookshelves with the other agriculture books.

In larger libraries it can be helpful if books are given a precise Dewey classification number. The teacher–librarian can find out the right classification number by deciding what the subject of the book is and then looking at the Junior Colour Code schedule in appendix 1 of this book. For example, a book on growing maize would now be given the classification number 633 and a red coloured spine label. Younger students may ignore the number, but it will help both older students and the teacher–librarian to use the library.

Under Dewey classification, history, geography and biography books are shelved together in the 900 (or 9) section. With the Junior Colour Code system history, geography and biography books are also kept together on the bookshelves, but they have blue labels on their spine to make it easier for students to find the books they are looking for. The table below shows the standard colours used in the Junior Colour Code system.

Junior Colour Code

Subject	Spine label colour	Dewey number
Reference	No colour	000
Philosophy, religion, festivals	Black	100 and 200
Transport and economics	Orange	300
Grammar, local languages	Brown	400
Science: physics, chemistry, maths, weather, rocks	Yellow	500–569
Biology: nature, animals	Green	570–599
Technology: agriculture, business, industry	Red	600
Art and sport, music	Purple	700
Literature: plays, poetry, myths, legends	Pink	800
History, geography, biography	Blue	900

- Copy this classification table on to a large poster so that students and staff can check where to look for books.

If you decide to use this classification method you will need to sort your books out, put a classification colour code on each spine label and then place the books on shelves with clear shelf guides.

If you have fewer than 500 information books and you decide you do not want to use the Junior Colour Code method of classifying books, we recommend that you divide the books up by timetable subject.

How to make spine labels

Once you know which subject your information book should be classified in and which classification system you are using, you will need to put a classification mark on a spine label on the outside cover of each book. Figure 7.1 shows how this is done. It is best to use a marker pen to write on the spine *or* stick coloured tape or masking tape on the spine and write the classification number on to the tape if appropriate. Some librarians write the number on a thin strip of paper and then glue this to the back cover, spine and front cover – however, this may not stay glued on if the book is borrowed regularly.

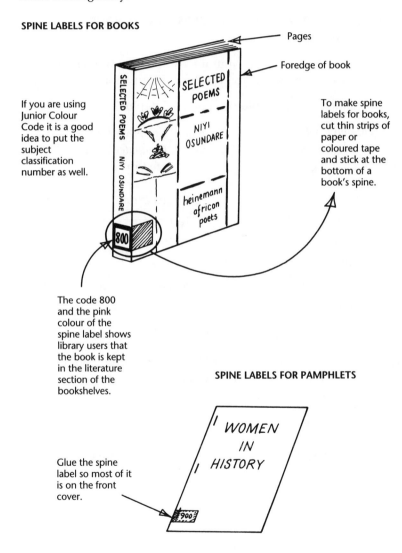

SPINE LABELS FOR BOOKS

Pages

Foredge of book

If you are using Junior Colour Code it is a good idea to put the subject classification number as well.

To make spine labels for books, cut thin strips of paper or coloured tape and stick at the bottom of a book's spine.

SELECTED POEMS
NIYI OSUNDARE
heinemann african poets

The code 800 and the pink colour of the spine label shows library users that the book is kept in the literature section of the bookshelves.

SPINE LABELS FOR PAMPHLETS

Glue the spine label so most of it is on the front cover.

WOMEN IN HISTORY

Figure 7.1 Putting spine labels on books and pamphlets

Teaching tip *Make a large subject index poster to guide students to the right subject area and bookshelves. If you are using Junior Colour Code, copy the classification table (on p. 54) and pin it up where everyone can see it.*

Make other posters to help students use the library. These should be large, easy to read and as attractive as possible. You could ask library club members to help you with this task.

Question-and-answer exercises to test your classifying skills

Q   If you decide to classify your library books by **timetable subject**, where would you file these information books?

What letter code would you put on the spine?

1	*Oil and Coal*	4	*Cooking with Eggs*
2	*Keeping Animals*	5	*Computer Skills*
3	*What is Rain?*	6	*Modern Poems*

A

Book title		Timetable subject	Code
1	*Oil and Coal*	Technology	TEC
2	*Keeping Animals*	Agriculture	AGRIC
3	*What is rain?*	Science	SCI
4	*Cooking with Eggs*	Home economics	HOME
5	*Computer Skills*	Business	BUS
6	*Modern Poems*	English	ENG

Q   If you decide to classify your library information books by **Junior Colour Code**, where would you place these books? What colour code would you put on the spine?

1	*Oil and Coal*	4	*Cooking with Eggs*
2	*Keeping Animals*	5	*Computer Skills*
3	*What is Rain?*	6	*Modern Poems*

A	Book title	Colour code	Subject code	Using the schedule
1	Oil and Coal	Red	600 Technology	622
2	Keeping Animals	Red	600 Technology	636
3	What is rain?	Yellow	500 Science	551.6
4	Cooking with Eggs	Red	600 Technology	641
5	Computer Skills	No colour	000 Reference	004
6	Modern Poems	Pink	800 Literature	821

What do you do when you have finished classification?

First – congratulations! Now that you have finished classifying the books in the library your remaining tasks are to make a shelf list, produce a title catalogue, organise the fiction books into alphabetical order and organise your lending system. Then you are ready to put the books on the shelves and open the school library.

8 Making library catalogues

What is a library catalogue?

A library catalogue tells you what books you have in your library and where to find them. Most library catalogues are arranged in alphabetical order.

Why make catalogues?

Your library may be small now, but if you are sent 1,000 gift books in the future you will need a catalogue so that you can find the book a student says he or she would like to read. Catalogues can be very helpful for teacher–librarians when they need to find information for the two questions most asked by library users:

1 Where can I find the book called . . .? (e.g. *Animal Farm* by George Orwell)

2 Is there any information in the library on . . .? (e.g. cyclones)

Different types of catalogue
In bigger libraries there will be several catalogues, including a title catalogue (and perhaps an author catalogue), a subject catalogue and a shelf list.

Title catalogues
A title catalogue helps you answer 'Is there a book in the library called . . .?' questions. This type of catalogue is useful because it is an alphabetical record of the titles of all the stock in the library. It is also essential for anyone who runs the library if you are ill, or if you leave the school.

Author catalogues
Some librarians recommend making an author catalogue. This is similar to a title catalogue, except that it is an alphabetical record of all the authors represented in the library. The problem is that some publications (especially pamphlets) do not have one obvious author. Because everything in your library will have a title, we recommend that you make a title catalogue and forget the author catalogue.

Subject catalogues

Subject catalogues help you answer the 'Is there any information in the library on . . .?' questions. However, subject catalogues can be complicated as they may need many cross-references to other subjects and titles. The simplest method, recommended for both primary and secondary school libraries, is to make a clear poster showing your classification system and to pin it up in the library as suggested on p. 54. Students can refer to the poster to find the books they need.

Shelf lists

A shelf list is a small file of cards arranged in the same order as the books on the shelves. The shelf list is a useful record for stocktaking (see p. 65), which is an essential task.

How do you make a title catalogue?

We recommend that you make a title catalogue record for every piece of stock in the library, from pamphlets to videos. Without a title record your successor, other staff and students may forget what titles are available in your library.

There are two ways of making a title catalogue: writing titles in an exercise book, or using a card index system. Both methods have been tried and tested by teacher–librarians, but the card index system is better if you are expecting your library to grow.

Title cataloguing using an exercise book
Figure 8.1 and the following step-by-step instructions explain how to make a title catalogue in an exercise book.

1   Divide each page of an exercise book into four columns, one for the title, one for the author (if known), one for the accession number and one for the subject classification – so that students know where to look for the book on the bookshelves.

2   Put all titles starting with A together on the same pages, all titles starting with B together on the same pages and so on until you reach Z. It does not matter if you mix information and fiction books on the same page.

The problem with this method is that as the page becomes full you cannot easily add new stock. However, it is a useful method if you cannot obtain catalogue cards and your library stock is small.

You need a separate page for each letter of the alphabet.

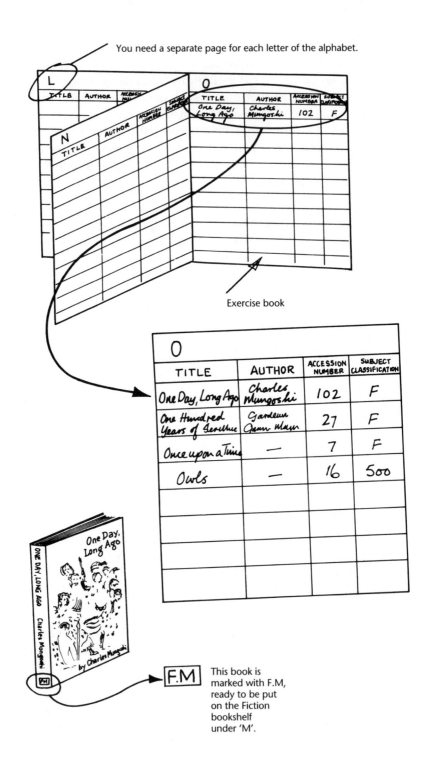

Exercise book

This book is marked with F.M, ready to be put on the Fiction bookshelf under 'M'.

Figure 8.1 Title catalogue in an exercise book

Title cataloguing using index cards

Figure 8.2 and the following instructions will explain how to make a title catalogue using index cards.

1   Each item of stock must have a separate card. If you are making your own index cards you should aim to make them a standard size – the ones available in shops and from library suppliers are 125 x 75 mm (5 x 3 inches).

2   On each index card write the title of the book at the top. Underneath write the author (if known). Beneath that write the accession number. Then on the line underneath write the subject classification if it is an information book, or F (for fiction) followed by a full stop and the first letter of the author's last name if is a fiction book. Users will then know where to find the book they want on the library shelves.

3   Keep the index cards filed in an issue box (this could be a shoe box) in alphabetical order by the title of the book. Show students how to use the title catalogue and explain that the index cards should never be removed from the issue box, nor should the order be muddled up.

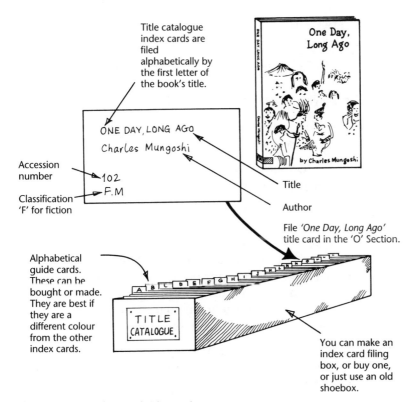

Title catalogue index cards are filed alphabetically by the first letter of the book's title.

Accession number

Classification 'F' for fiction

Title

Author

File 'One Day, Long Ago' title card in the 'O' Section.

Alphabetical guide cards. These can be bought or made. They are best if they are a different colour from the other index cards.

You can make an index card filing box, or buy one, or just use an old shoebox.

Figure 8.2 An index card title catalogue

61

How do you make a subject index?

The best way to make a simple subject index is to draw a poster. If you are using the Junior Colour Code classification scheme in your library you could copy the table below on to a poster or you could make a poster of the Tree of Knowledge illustrated in chapter 14 (figure 14.2).

Junior Colour Code

Subject	Spine label colour	Code number
Reference	No colour	000
Philosophy, religion, festivals	Black	100 and 200
Transport and economics	Orange	300
Grammar, local languages	Brown	400
Science: physics, chemistry, maths, weather, rocks	Yellow	500-569
Biology: nature, animals	Green	570-599
Technology: agriculture, business, industry	Red	600
Art and sport, music	Purple	700
Literature: plays, poetry, myths, legends	Pink	800
History, geography biography	Blue	900

How do you make a shelf list?

Every information and fiction book needs a shelf list card. Use standard sized index cards.

1   Take a book. On the top left-hand side of the index card put the book's subject code or classification number.

    a)   If it is an information book (e.g. *Try the Rabbit* by Stephan Adjare, which is about breeding rabbits for meat in Ghana) this may be a number (e.g. 600 or 6), the subject (e.g. agriculture) or the colour reference (e.g. red). Look at chapter 7 again to remind yourself about classification. You do not need to put all three classification codes, but it is important to be consistent and to use whatever method you have decided on every time.

    b)   If it is a fiction book (e.g. *Moses in a Mess* by Barbara Kimenye) there will be no classification code. Instead write 'F.K'. The F stands for fiction and is obviously quicker to write on each of the shelf list cards than the full word 'fiction'. After the full stop you write K, for Kimenye, which is the first letter of the author's surname.

2 Underneath the classification code or F letter, write the title of the book.

3 Underneath the title, write the name of the author, if known.

4 At the bottom right-hand corner, write the book's accession number.

5 Arrange shelf list cards for information books by their subject classification number. Arrange shelf list cards for fiction books in alphabetical order by the author's last name.

6 When you have a card for all the books, take each card and make two holes in the left side – you could do this with a hole punch. Put some string through this hole and tie all the cards for each subject into a booklet. Make a separate booklet for the fiction titles.

7 If you are using the simple Dewey Decimal Classification or Junior Colour Code classification (see chapter 7) your shelf list for information books will now be divided into ten booklets. These can be used when you stocktake.

8 If your library receives more books you can untie the string and add shelf list cards for the new stock.

Figures 8.3 and 8.4 show what a shelf list card and a shelf list catalogue (or booklet) should look like.

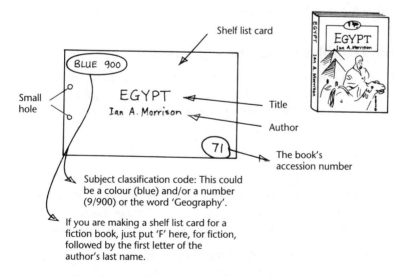

Figure 8.3 Making a shelf list card

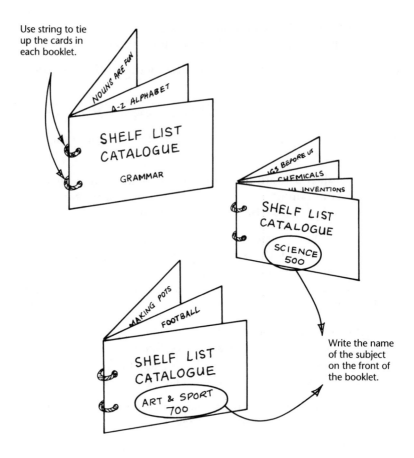

Use string to tie up the cards in each booklet.

NOUNS ARE FUN
A-Z ALPHABET
SHELF LIST CATALOGUE
GRAMMAR

...GS BEFORE US
CHEMICALS
...L INVENTIONS
SHELF LIST CATALOGUE
SCIENCE 500

...KING POTS
FOOTBALL
SHELF LIST CATALOGUE
ART & SPORT 700

Write the name of the subject on the front of the booklet.

Figure 8.4 Shelf list catalogues

How to solve some cataloguing problems

- **Takes a long time?**   You will probably find making catalogues is quite easy to do, but that it takes a long time. Try and encourage students to help you make these catalogues.

- **Hard to read?**   Write neatly. You could use a typewriter if one is available.

- **Two or more copies of the same book?**   Write a separate title card and shelf list card for each of these books. You will be able to tell that there is more than one copy because the accession number (in the bottom right-hand corner) will be different.

- **Authors who have written more than one book?**   File these by their classification number, then alphabetically by the title of the book.

What is stocktaking?

Stocktaking is done to find out if all stock in the library is still
there. For security reasons at the end of every term ask students
and staff to return all their books to the library. But once a year,
near the end of the final term when some students will be leaving
the school for ever, close the library for a day for a stocktake. Ask
library monitors or club members to walk round the bookshelves
using the shelf list to check that the information and fiction books
are all on the shelves. This is how a teacher working for VSO in
Sierra Leone taught her counterparts and students to stocktake:

*'Take the shelf list booklet and check each book, shelf by shelf. If books
are missing, write "missing" and the date in the space below the titles.
Also mark with red ink the outer edge of the shelf list booklet so that
missing books can be easily traced when flicking through the shelf list
booklet later.'*

*'If the books are there, leave the space on the shelf list card empty. When
the books are checked and found to be there, turn them 45 degrees, so
that they are fore-edge down on the shelf. Then any books which are left
upright are either in the wrong place; or have no shelf list card or have
been missed in the stocktake checking.'*
Christine George, Sierra Leone

Pin up notices so that students and staff know which books are
missing. Encourage people to return missing books, using the ideas
suggested in chapter 11.

9 Alphabetical filing

What is filed alphabetically in the library?

Alphabetical filing is used for many library tasks. Most libraries arrange fiction books alphabetically on the shelves using the author's last name (sometimes called surname). Alphabetical filing can also be used to organise index cards and borrowers' cards in a logical and easy-to-find order.

Why file alphabetically?

Filing books alphabetically keeps them in order. It means that anyone who knows the alphabet can find any fiction book they want in any library. Alphabetical filing is a system you can teach students easily.

How do you file alphabetically?

To file alphabetically you must put items in A to Z order, starting at A and finishing with Z. It is essential that students, from the first-formers through to the library monitors, know their A to Z and are very confident about alphabetical filing. It is useful to check this, perhaps by using a set of cards, and also to do some of the learning games suggested in the teaching tips at the end of this chapter, before the library opens. This will help students understand how stock is organised in the library and may encourage some to help the teacher–librarian return books to the right bookshelves.

Putting fiction books in alphabetical order
To arrange fiction books alphabetically on the shelves, put all the books written by authors with last names starting with A on the same shelf. Then do the same with all the books written by authors with the last names starting with B, then all the Cs, and so on. Keep on dividing like this until you reach Z.

Use shelf guides (see chapter 10) with large letters on, to show clearly where the A section, for example, starts. Figure 9.1 shows what your fiction bookshelves should look like.

To help keep your fiction books in alphabetical order when you put them on the bookshelves it is useful to give them a spine label (see chapter 7). The spine label can be glued or taped on. It should

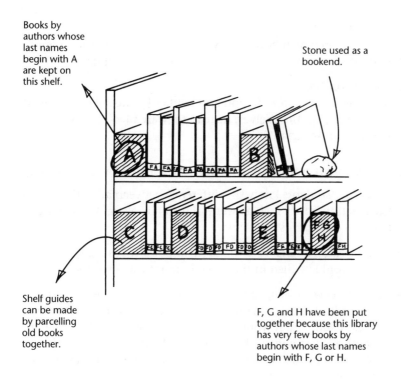

Books by authors whose last names begin with A are kept on this shelf.

Stone used as a bookend.

Shelf guides can be made by parcelling old books together.

F, G and H have been put together because this library has very few books by authors whose last names begin with F, G or H.

Figure 9.1 Fiction books arranged alphabetically on shelves

have an F for fiction and the first letter of the author's last name. For example, a novel by R.K. Narayan should have its spine label clearly marked with F.N. Until students become used to the system you may find some books are wrongly filed in the F section.

Some librarians like to put fiction books in alphabetical order using the first two letters of the author's last name. This means that if there are several authors in the S section they are then arranged in alphabetical order from the second letter: SAdd should go before SMith, because A comes before M. You can do this if you want to, but at most primary or secondary schools there is no need. Simply see which letter of the alphabet the author's last name starts with and then file the book in that section on the bookshelves, so that, for example, *A Man of the People*, written by Chinua Achebe, will be filed with books by authors whose surnames start with A.

Filing other items alphabetically
Title catalogues
In all libraries, the index cards in title catalogues should be alphabetically filed by the title of the book. Also, if you choose to have an author catalogue in your library, the index cards should be alphabetically filed by the author's last name.

Borrower cards

Depending on which borrower system you have chosen for your library, students' borrower cards may also be filed alphabetically.

Information books

Information books (non-fiction and textbooks) are *not* usually filed alphabetically on the shelves. Instead they are filed by subject classification (see chapter 7).

How do you avoid problems with alphabetical filing?

- Make sure students know the difference between an author and a title. Fiction books such as *Matigari* (title) by Ngugi Wa Thiong'o (author) can confuse students.

- Assume small letters have the same importance as big letters (e.g. d'Argy would be filed in the D section, not the A section).

- For authors who seem to have several names, like James Hadley Chase or Ruth Prawer Jhabvala, file books under their last name. In these examples, it would be C for Chase and J for Jhabvala. If the author's last name is hyphenated, like Wu Ch'eng-en, the book would be filed under the first letter of the <u>whole</u> last name, in this case C.

- If your library has two copies of the same book, file them together. If the library has several different books written by the same author, then file them alphabetically by the book title as well. For example: the title of Maya Angelou's *All God's Children Need Travelling Shoes* starts with an A and so it should be put on the bookshelf in front of *I Know Why The Caged Bird Sings*, also by Maya Angelou, which starts with an I.

- Some books have titles which start with a number, for example *100 Gifts to Make*. It is recommended that you think of this title as starting with a word, not a number – so it would be filed under O for One Hundred.

- Ignore 'A', 'An' and 'The' at the beginning of a title and file the book by the first letter of the next word.

....

Teaching tips   *Help your students to learn the A to Z rules of alphabetical filing with these games.*

    1 Alphabetical library words   *Divide the class into two teams. Then ask students to think of some library words such as book, story, page, shelf, etc. See which team is the first to find library words for every letter of the alphabet, starting at A and trying to reach Z.*

2 **Alphabetical bookmarks** Ask students to make a bookmark (see chapter 14) with their first name written clearly on it, and then to decorate it. When they have finished ask students to arrange the bookmarks in alphabetical order.

3 **Organising books in alphabetical order** Here are some books arranged alphabetically on the fiction bookshelf.

Fiction books arranged alphabetically

Figure 9.2 Organising books in alphabetical order – an exercise

Now draw some pretend books, in muddled order, on the chalkboard and see if students can work out the alphabetical order they should go in.

4 **More bookmarks** Ask students to draw another bookmark, this time putting their first and second name – Nelly Collin, for example. Divide the class into four teams and ask students to arrange their bookmarks in alphabetical order from the surname. Which letter of the alphabet is the most popular? This might be a good time to play the **Authors game** (see chapter 14).

At the end of this teaching session students will know more about alphabetical filing and will have two bookmarks. Remind students that bookmarks help you remember which page you have reached in the book you are reading. Using a bookmark also stops students from bending the corners of pages to mark the place they have reached – a habit that spoils books and can result in torn and lost pages.

10 Putting books on shelves

The essential tasks for setting up a school library are nearly complete: putting books on shelves is one of the final steps.

What needs to be checked?

Before you start to fill your shelves, make sure that every book has:

- an individual accession number and entry in the accession register
- a school nameplate and return date label glued at the front of the book. The school's name should also be stamped in one or two more places inside the book
- a spine label
- a shelf list card
- a title card.

If you have missed out any of these procedures, it is recommended that you complete them now – before you start to put books on the library shelves.

What are the best bookshelves?

Look again at chapter 3 and study the illustrations showing how to make the best bookshelves. If your school does not have funds to make or buy new bookcases it is recommended that you use some type of display container. Wooden packing cases, for example, are very suitable and should not be too difficult to obtain. Chris Lane, working in Kenya, has a warning for anyone making furniture for their library:

'Bookshelves should be at a suitable height for your pupils. It is a common fault to make them too high. Wall shelves can be taller than free-standing shelves, which should be kept low to give a feeling of space. The air must be free to circulate around books. This will cut down on mould and problems with insects.'

If you do not have a separate room for your library you will need to lock up books in a cupboard or box when the room is unsupervised. Some teacher–librarians recommend using lockable, glass-fronted bookcases; these stop books being stolen, but allow students to see what texts are available.

Why use bookshelves?

Bookshelves have many uses.

- They organise the library's stock so that it is easy to find books.

- If books are not being used and are stored badly they can become damaged – a box of books could be eaten by insects or mice.

- A shelf of books is much easier for you to check.

- Bookshelves can help prevent water damage if there is a flood.

- Bookshelves can also be used to display magazines, project boxes and audio-visual stock.

How do you use bookshelves?

Throughout the world people use bookshelves in a certain way. Your students may not realise this, so tell them that books are put on the top shelf first and then filed from left to right. Fiction books are placed on bookshelves in alphabetical order. This means that if you have an empty bookcase, books by authors whose last names start with A will be put on the left-hand side of the top shelf.

Remember to keep the spines facing out and the writing on them easy to read. This means the title, author and publisher's symbol will be running from the top of the spine to the bottom. Students may need plenty of practice arranging books on shelves before they are confident about doing it correctly.

As one VSO teacher in Kenya found:

'I have spent the past year trying to teach students that books are placed on shelves with the spine facing outwards, not inwards.'

If you have enough books to fill two bookcases you should use the bookcase on the left (as you look at it) first. Arrange the books on the top shelf, filling each shelf from left to right down to the bottom until every shelf is full. Then put books on the other bookcase, starting at the top shelf.

Teaching tip *If your bookshelves are too tightly packed with books, it will be hard for students to take a book off the shelf. On the other hand, if the books are arranged too loosely they will start leaning and then fall down. One way to overcome this problem is to make some L-shaped bookends, or use a large stone, for books to lean against.*

Solving shelving problems

Problems	Solutions
1 If the library has only one bookcase, it may be too crowded for students to browse when a whole form comes to the library together.	Have more bookcases and make them lower.
2 If every student borrows a book, there may be no books left on the shelves.	Lend one book at a time to students for one week. Make sure that books are returned. Use book ends or stones to keep books from falling out of order on the shelf.
3. Students may not understand how to find books, or may not remember to return books to the shelves.	Explain how the bookcases work. Show students the shelf guide signs and look at the ideas for student education in chapters 6 and 14.

How to help students use bookshelves the right way
Students may forget to put books back on the shelf the right way round. Remind them to put the books back in the correct place with the spine facing outwards, as shown in figure 10.1. Explain that this is so that other borrowers can easily find the book they want by reading the title and author information printed on the spine.

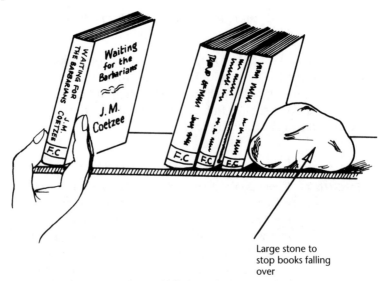

Large stone to stop books falling over

Figure 10.1 Putting books on a shelf the right way

What is a shelf guide?

A tour guide is a person who shows tourists the main places of interest and beauty around your country. In a way, a shelf guide is similar! It is a guide (or small sign) that helps library users find the books they want to read.

Making shelf guides

Shelf guides are essential and can be made in many ways.

1   Paint the name of the type of book (e.g. reference) on the shelf. This may be best for a secondary school library, especially if you have some good artists. But the disadvantage is that as your collection grows the guide may be in the wrong place, so you will have to paint over it and then paint the word again on the right part of the bookshelf.

2   Another method is to stencil the subject name (e.g. agriculture) with marker pens on to a piece of strong paper, and then pin it on to the shelves. This is a good method, but the problem is that it may get torn, or fall down. Figure 10.2 shows this type of shelf guide.

3   If you have very old or torn books you can parcel two books of the same size together and use them as shelf guides. Just draw the letter of the alphabet, or the classification code, on to the parcel. You can see examples of these in figure 9.1 in chapter 9. This is an easy way for students to find out what they are looking for, and the shelf guides are easy to move to the right place when your stock grows.

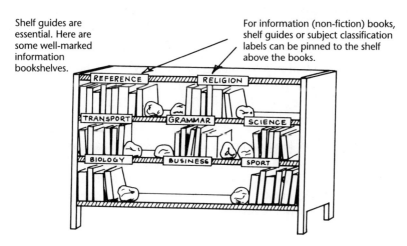

Shelf guides are essential. Here are some well-marked information bookshelves.

For information (non-fiction) books, shelf guides or subject classification labels can be pinned to the shelf above the books.

Figure 10.2 Shelf guide for information (non-fiction) bookshelves

11 Lending books

It is essential to think carefully about the type of lending system that will work best at your school. It is recommended that you discuss these ideas with the library committee as soon as you can. Once a decision is made you will then be able to make the appropriate return date labels or prepare exercise books (see chapter 6). Putting the finishing touches to your lending system is the final step in the list of essential tasks recommended by this book when you set up a school library. When the lending system has been prepared the library can open and books can be lent.

What does lending books mean?

Lending books means students and staff can take fiction or information books away from the library (in other words, borrow them) for a set time to read or study on their own.

Some students find borrowing books confusing. If students are having problems understanding, explain that to be lent a book by the library or to borrow a book means to take it for a short time and then to return it by a set date. The teacher–librarian or library monitors should only lend books to students who return their books, in good condition, to the library by the day stamped (or written) on the return date label.

Reference books, like encyclopaedias and dictionaries, should not be lent. Instead encourage students to use reference books in the library. Make sure these books have the library's nameplate glued or rubber-stamped inside them to avoid arguments about ownership.

Lending books will involve making guidelines for the borrowers. It is best to put up a poster, near the librarian's desk, so that students can easily remember the rules (see figure 11.1). Figure 11.2 shows a model set of borrowing rules.

Three methods of lending books are described in this chapter. You need only choose one of these methods. It is recommended that you discuss which would be best for your school with the library committee. Remember that you have to decide on your method well before you actually open the library.

Figure 11.1 Rules for borrowing books displayed in a library in Solomon Islands

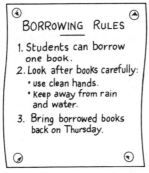

BORROWING RULES

1. Students can borrow one book.
2. Look after books carefully:
   • use clean hands.
   • keep away from rain and water.
3. Bring borrowed books back on Thursday.

Figure 11.2 A poster showing borrowing rules in a school library

Three methods of lending books are described in this chapter. You need only choose one of these methods. It is recommended that you discuss which would be best for your school with the library committee. Remember that you have to decide on your method well before you actually open the library.

Why lend books?

Lending fiction and information books supports the literacy and education work of the school, allowing students to study or read in their own time. If your library has restricted opening hours students may feel frustrated because they do not have enough time to finish finding the information they want. It is widely accepted that students who regularly read books and magazines find their school work easier.

Some students may be keen to borrow books but will need the teacher–librarian's help to find a suitable book at the right level so that they can enjoy reading it without supervision or repeatedly having to look up words in a dictionary.

'They are keen readers of library books but some need help to choose books of a suitable standard to stretch their ability.'
Lucy Hamilton, Pal Malmal High School, Papua New Guinea

How do you decide borrowing rules?

To avoid losing books through confusion about lending or borrowing and to avoid causing bad feeling, we recommend that you decide some basic library rules before allowing students to borrow books. It is best if you make these decisions with your library committee.

Decide how many books each student can borrow
One book is probably enough, especially if you do not have a large stock at your library.

Decide how long a student can keep a borrowed book
A week is about the right length of time for most students to read a book of their choice. It might be easier for the teacher–librarian if all books are returned on the same day of the week, for example Thursday, especially if this is the day when the library club meets. Then library club members can help put books back on the shelves.

Decide whether to charge fines
Some librarians worry that if they lend books, a few will not be returned to the library by the correct date, as stamped or written on the return date label. That is why they ask for a small fee for every day a book is kept out of the library after the day it is due back. This is charging a fine.

The longer the delay before the book is returned the more money the borrower will owe. No other books can be borrowed by that person until they pay their library fine. The aim is that students and staff will dislike paying fines so they will remember to return the book they have borrowed on the correct day. If you tell people that they can borrow the book again if they have not finished it, they may also be encouraged to return the book on the day stamped (or written) in the date label.

Fines are useful because everyone is treated the same way and the money raised can help to pay for book repairs and new titles.

However, many librarians have found that fines cause problems because people are confused by the idea. Nicole Fitton, working as a library adviser in Bangladesh, warns:

'Be careful of fines. It may create more work, administrative problems and bad feeling.'

If you decide to charge fines for overdue, lost or damaged books, make sure you explain the rules well and make a simple-to-understand poster. You may also find that keeping money, even very small amounts, in the library is a problem. You will need a lockable drawer or a lockable cash box to keep the fine money securely.

Decide what to do about lost or damaged books

There are some well tested ways of making sure missing library books are returned to the library. If you know a student has not yet returned the book they borrowed, try these ideas:

1   If the book is late and you have a fine system you should try and encourage the student who borrowed the book to find it, and return it to the library soon. Library monitors could help you do this.

2   Send a message to the form requesting the student to return the book to the library.

3   Give each form teacher a list of books that are missing from the library. Ask the teacher to make students look for these titles, in their formroom, dormitories or home, and to return them.

4   Ask the head teacher to read out the names of the students who your records show have not returned books.

5   If you find some students regularly spoiling or losing books, despite form lessons and individual help from the teacher–librarian, try keeping a list of students who are temporarily not allowed to borrow books.

'This acted as a real deterrent for other kids, and as time passed their names could be removed from the list of problem students so that they could be given a second chance at the librarian's discretion.'
Liz Platt, working in Zanzibar with colleagues Halima Khamis Hamad and Wanu Amour

6   Finally, ask the library committee to recommend that the head teacher does not award end-of-term certificates until all books are returned or accounted for.

How do you record books lent by the library?

First of all, before lending any library stock it is essential that all information books and fiction books have a return date label glued into the front and the name of the school written in one or more places inside the book. The book should also have an accession number, a shelf list card, a title card and a spine label. Look back at chapters 6–8 if you have not yet completed any of these tasks. You can choose from three alternative methods of recording which books are lent by the library. Decide with the committee which would be best at your school.

Lending using an exercise book

To make a simple record of who has borrowed what items from the library use a big exercise book, with ruled columns as shown in figure 11.3. If your school has many students you might prefer to write this information in a different book for each form.

Every time someone borrows a book from the library, write down in the exercise book:

• the student's name
• the book's name/title
• the author
• the classification code (or fiction code) on the spine label
• the date the book is due back.

The advantage with this method is that it is very quick to set up. It is particularly good for primary school students.

The disadvantage is that it takes a long time to use. You or the duty librarian will have to write in all the information for every book that is borrowed. It is also hard to trace who has borrowed which books and which ones are returned late, because the borrowers' names are not written down alphabetically.

None the less, this method of borrowing books is excellent for a formroom library. One adaptation you could make is to give every student their own page in the borrowers' exercise book. This is useful for English teachers who wish to see how well a student is progressing with their reading.

Lending using borrower cards

This is a useful lending method because students' borrower cards are filed alphabetically and so are easy to find in the issue box. You can also work with several library monitors to record books going out on loan at the same time.

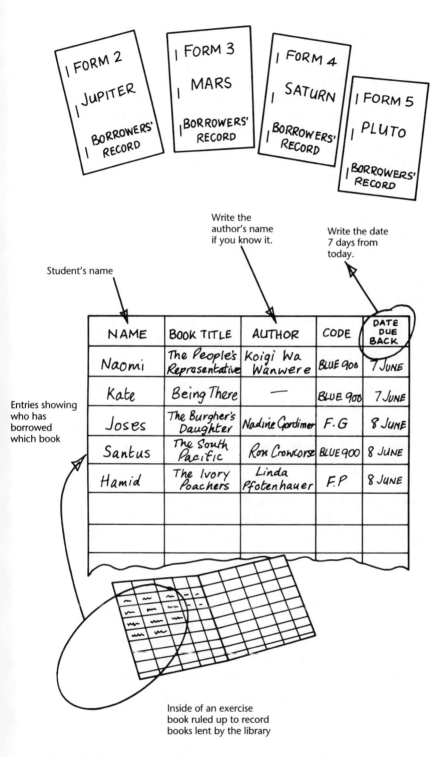

Inside of an exercise
book ruled up to record
books lent by the library

Figure 11.3 An example of the exercise book system of recording books
lent by the library

The borrower card

Students who want to borrow books must have a borrower card. This is a stiff piece of card. The standard size issue card sold in shops is about 125 x 75 mm (5 x 3 inches). At the top, in large letters, the teacher–librarian or the library monitor should write the student's name. Below the student's name, rule four columns where the title of the book the student wishes to borrow can be written together with other information, such as the author, reference number and due-back date. Figure 11.4 shows a borrower card and how it fits into the borrower card system of lending books.

The issue box

Borrowers do not keep their borrower card. When they want to borrow a book they take the book (or other item of stock) to the library desk. The librarian then finds their borrower card, which will be arranged alphabetically in the issue box (or shoe box), and writes in the relevant information on the card.

The issue box is divided into two sections by stiff pieces of coloured card (see figure 11.4). At one end, marked STUDENTS, are borrower cards belonging to students who do not have a book out of the library at the moment; and at the other end, under BOOKS OUT, are borrower cards with up-to-date information about which books are currently on loan and to whom.

The librarian must ask if the student has a book out on loan. If the answer is 'yes' the librarian will ask for the book, look for the student's borrower card in the BOOKS OUT section and then cross out the entry to show the book has been returned.

If the student does not have a book on loan, then the librarian will find their borrower card in the STUDENTS section of the issue box. He or she will then stamp the return date (say seven days from that day) on the return date label at the front of the book *and* on the student's borrower card.

One day a week the librarian could go through the BOOKS OUT section of the issue box to see which books and pamphlets are now due for return. Mark the cards that show students are late returning library books with a paper clip. Alternatively, keep such cards in groups by form and then at the end of each term go through the cards to see if any books are still outstanding.

The disadvantage of this borrowing system is that cards are quite easy to lose. It is also still quite slow for the teacher–librarian and library monitors to process, because you need to write out information about the book on each borrower card. If there are problems with books being returned late you may also find it hard to discover which students are keeping books longer than allowed.

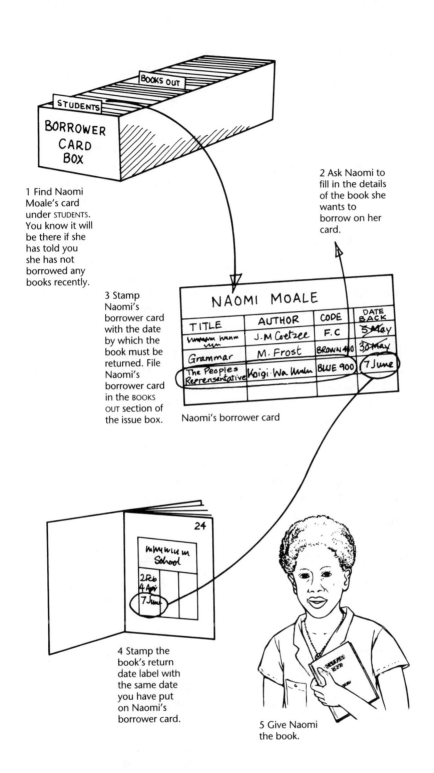

BORROWER CARD BOX

STUDENTS

BOOKS OUT

1 Find Naomi Moale's card under STUDENTS. You know it will be there if she has told you she has not borrowed any books recently.

2 Ask Naomi to fill in the details of the book she wants to borrow on her card.

3 Stamp Naomi's borrower card with the date by which the book must be returned. File Naomi's borrower card in the BOOKS OUT section of the issue box.

NAOMI MOALE

TITLE	AUTHOR	CODE	DATE BACK
ᴠᴠᴠᴠᴠ ᴠᴠᴠ	J.M Coetzee	F.C	5 May
Grammar	M. Frost	BROWN 400	30 May
The Peoples Representative	Koigi Wa Waml	BLUE 900	7 June

Naomi's borrower card

24

ᴠᴠᴠᴠᴠ ᴠᴠᴠ School

2 Feb
4 Apr
7 June

4 Stamp the book's return date label with the same date you have put on Naomi's borrower card.

5 Give Naomi the book.

Figure 11.4 The borrower card system of recording books lent by the library

Lending using a book ticket system

This is an excellent borrowing system for a secondary school, especially if you expect students to be borrowing one or more books each week.

Book pockets and book tickets

Every book needs a book pocket and a book ticket. The book pocket can be made of strong paper, and you can make it at the same time as you make the school's nameplate. Alternatively, you can buy book pockets from library suppliers.

If you are making separate book pockets, then glue them at the front of the book on the title page. You do not need a lot of glue to stick them into the book – just paste the glue on a thin 25 mm (1 inch) strip at the top of each book pocket. Some people like to glue them on the inside back cover; there is no right or wrong way, but make sure you are consistent. Look back at chapter 6, and figure 6.2, for more details about making and sticking book pockets.

Next you need to make a book ticket from strong card. The ticket should be tall enough to be seen when it is inside the book pocket: a recommended size is 6 cm x 10 cm ($2^1/_2$ x 4 inches). A good way to obtain free paper or card is to ask print companies (printers) if you can have any paper offcuts. Most will be happy to help.

On each book ticket, write the title of the book, its classification code or number and its accession number. Then rule two columns. One will be for the student's name and the other for the date the book is due back (see figure 11.5). All this should not take up more than 5 cm (2 inches) of the book ticket, so that there is plenty of space left for recording borrowings.

Finally, put the book ticket into its book pocket.

Making a date return tray

When someone borrows a book under the book ticket system, they do not take the ticket away with the book. This means that you have to make or find a narrow issue box, or date return tray, in which to store book tickets from books which are being borrowed. You can see such a box in figure 11.5. You will need to make a card for each day of the month from 1 through to 31 and also a card for each month from January to December to go in the box or tray. Make these cards using stiff coloured paper. They should be a little taller then the book tickets.

How to borrow books under the book ticket system

When a student borrows a book the teacher–librarian will ask them to write their name in the appropriate column on the book ticket.

This is what the FRONT and BACK of a book ticket look like when it has been ruled up.

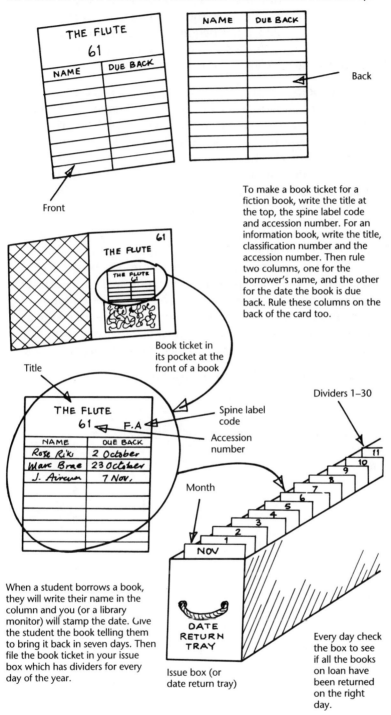

Front

Back

To make a book ticket for a fiction book, write the title at the top, the spine label code and accession number. For an information book, write the title, classification number and the accession number. Then rule two columns, one for the borrower's name, and the other for the date the book is due back. Rule these columns on the back of the card too.

Book ticket in its pocket at the front of a book

Title

Spine label code

Accession number

Month

Dividers 1–30

When a student borrows a book, they will write their name in the column and you (or a library monitor) will stamp the date. Give the student the book telling them to bring it back in seven days. Then file the book ticket in your issue box which has dividers for every day of the year.

Issue box (or date return tray)

Every day check the box to see if all the books on loan have been returned on the right day.

Figure 11.5 The book ticket system of recording books lent by the library

The student does this, then gives the book ticket to the teacher–librarian who files it in the date return tray, alphabetically by the title of the book if it is fiction, or in numerical sequence (or colour) according to its classification code if it is an information book, under the date when it is to be returned.

Returned books

When a student returns a book the teacher–librarian must look to see what date was last stamped on the return date label. Then, looking at the title of the book, she or he must look for the book's individual book ticket in the section of the issue box or date return tray that contains the book tickets, arranged in order, for books due back on that day – for example, in the May section, under 5, if the student's book is due to be returned on 5 May.

The advantages with this method are that it is very quick when students want to borrow books and it is very easy to see which books have been returned late, and by whom. The book ticket system takes time to set up, because you must make a nameplate with a book pocket, a book ticket for every information (non-fiction) and fiction title in the library (except reference books) and cards for the issue box, so it is recommended that you encourage the library monitors or library club members to help you.

You can now open your library doors and lend books!

12 Keeping books in good condition

Why keep books in good condition?

Books are made of paper, which is a delicate material prone to damage – particularly in tropical climates. This means books will be easily spoilt if they are stored carelessly or handled roughly. Books are also difficult and expensive to obtain in school libraries throughout the world. For these two reasons it is important to take extra care to keep books in good condition.

What does keeping books in good condition involve?

To keep library books in good condition the teacher–librarian must anticipate problems. These range from coping with adverse weather conditions to pest infestation in the library.

The simple methods work best. The library committee should ensure the library is secure and weatherproof. Stop students from eating in the library, and try to sweep the floor and dust shelves regularly. You could encourage library monitors to make a rota so that some cleaning jobs are done every day in the library.

S. M. Abdullah, working at Mombasa Industrial Training Centre, Kenya believes:

'The cleanliness of a library is important. Nothing is more dispiriting than walking into a library where the books and shelves are covered with dust and it is necessary to wipe the chair and table with a handkerchief before sitting down. When you have been dumped in the small room, commonly known as a "library" (just because it contains books for the school) you will see that keeping a library clean is not easy.'

How to cope with water
In most countries there are certain seasons when bad weather can be expected. Be aware of changes and listen to the radio for news about monsoons and flooding. Water can be the library's biggest enemy. Make sure that:

- the roof does not leak, as even a small drip can damage your stock beyond repair
- gutters are kept clear

85

- windows have shutters or louvres which can be closed when the weather is bad
- storm water cannot flow into the library
- books are kept on shelves at least 15 cm (6 inches) above the ground, so that if water collects in the library there is less chance of books being damaged – and time to put the stock on higher shelves. The 15 cm (6 inch) space is also useful because it is high enough to allow you to sweep under the bookshelves and keep the library clean.

How to cope with humidity

In tropical countries the wet season and general humidity encourages mould to grow on books, papers and audio-visual stock. If you are lucky and have electricity you could try and budget for ceiling fans. Books suffer if kept in a room with unreliable air-conditioning because of the repeated changes in humidity.

It is important to make sure plenty of fresh air can circulate. Leave the door and windows open during the day. If you have made a formroom library, in a lockable cupboard, it is essential that the books are handled regularly to ensure they do not collect dust and are exposed to fresh air. The easiest way to do this is to give students as much opportunity as possible to look at the books.

Audio-visual equipment lasts longer if it is kept in an air-conditioned room because it is easily spoiled by humidity and mould. Store tapes, films and videos in a dry, clean place, preferably in an airtight container with silica gel.

How to stop insect damage

Insects may be small but they can cause a lot of damage. Some insects, like cockroaches, mosquitoes and red and black ants do not spoil books – but they do upset students. These insects can be killed with insect sprays on sale locally. The sprays are powerful so instructions should be followed carefully. It is best to use them at the end of the day when the library is empty.

White ants are difficult to remove and have destroyed many library collections. One tip is to varnish or paint shelves, and if possible treat them chemically, before you put books on to them.

Always look out for signs of insect damage, and take action against insects as soon as you can.

'The best way to discourage insects (like termites, silverfish bookworms, etc.) apart from insecticides is to make sure that the books are used a

*great deal and are dusted and wiped (with a dry cloth) regularly. The
shelves must be kept clean and polished.'*
Christine George, in her unpublished handbook for secondary
school teacher–librarians in Sierra Leone

If you see a book or magazine that looks as if 'someone' has been
eating it, remove the book at once. Silverfish bookworms should
be killed. You can shake them out of the book and then stand on
them. If white ants come to your library then pay for chemical
treatment as soon as possible. If you delay the ants may destroy all
your books and even the building.

*'We were so proud of our bookshelves and the magazine display rack.
They looked so smart with all the stock piled up high. It was really nice
for a year and then the white ants moved in. In less than two months all
our journalism books, pamphlet collection and magazines had become
food for insects – and worse, the office building had to be partly rebuilt.'*
Jennifer Aiwewe and Joseph Aihunu, journalists working at
Solomon Islands Development Trust with the author

Insects cannot eat metal bookshelves. However, if you have metal
bookshelves you may have problems with rust, which also spoils
books. The rule is to keep everything clean and to anticipate
trouble.

How to remove rodents
Animals like rats and mice can damage your bookshelves and
stock. You could put down traps to kill them, or use a specially
made poison (but be sure to follow the instructions very carefully
and store the poison in a safe place). Or you could borrow a cat. If
you suspect your library is the home of rodents, act quickly. The
best method is the one you would use in your own home.

How to handle books carefully
Damage caused by borrowers may also be a major problem. Books
will stay in better condition if you teach students how to hold and
use stock carefully.

The weakest area of a book is its spine. If this breaks, all the pages
will fall out. Teach students to open books carefully. If spines look
weak, strengthen them with strong sticky tape inside and outside
the cover. The spine may also be damaged if the librarian stamps
the date label too enthusiastically. One reason why librarians tend
to glue the date label at the front of the book, rather than at the
back, is so that they can stamp a page which has the padding of
other pages behind it. You may also find that it is a good idea to
cover books with a dust jacket (cover) of sticky-back plastic or
strong paper. Figure 12.1 shows you how to do this.

Arrange library lessons so that you can show students how to read books without damaging the spine or tearing the pages, and explain why they should use bookmarks.

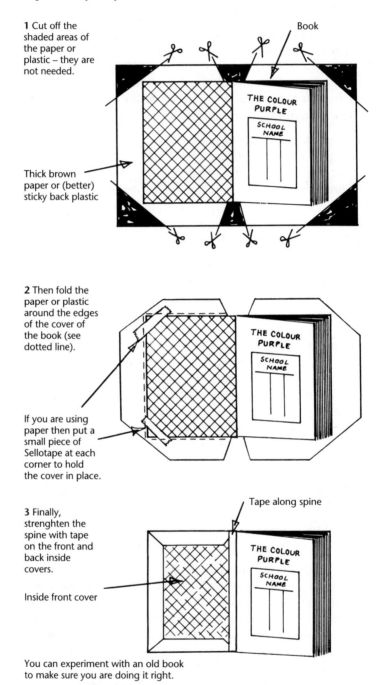

1 Cut off the shaded areas of the paper or plastic – they are not needed.

Book

THE COLOUR PURPLE

SCHOOL NAME

Thick brown paper or (better) sticky back plastic

2 Then fold the paper or plastic around the edges of the cover of the book (see dotted line).

If you are using paper then put a small piece of Sellotape at each corner to hold the cover in place.

THE COLOUR PURPLE

SCHOOL NAME

Tape along spine

3 Finally, strenghten the spine with tape on the front and back inside covers.

Inside front cover

THE COLOUR PURPLE

SCHOOL NAME

You can experiment with an old book to make sure you are doing it right.

Figure 12.1 How to cover a book with plastic/paper

How do you repair damaged stock?

The most common damage is a broken spine. Use a rubber-based glue, like Copydex, which is slightly stretchy even when it dries, to glue the spine securely back into place.

If a hardback book has loose pages you could glue them back into place. Try to avoid using Sellotape because it dries, shrinks and then falls off. It can also stain books a yellow-brown colour. But, if there is nothing else, then use Sellotape or Scotch 3M Magic Tape to secure the pages. Figure 12.2 shows how to repair a book with glue.

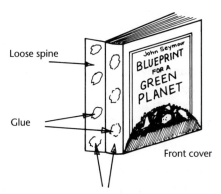

Spread glue thinly on both surfaces. Then press the surface together. Wait until the glue has dried (about 24 hours) before putting the book back on the shelves. Covering a book after gluing it would give it extra protection.

Figure 12.2 How to repair a book with glue

There are other methods of fixing loose pages back into books. For paperbacks you may prefer to staple the pages together again with a giant stapler. If you are mending a thin pamphlet you could try making a series of about eight or ten holes 4 mm (one eighth of an inch) from the spine using a hole punch and then secure the pages with string.

Most teacher librarians find their own way of mending books.

S. M. Abdullah, working at the Mombasa Industrial Training Centre, advises:

'A book which is torn and falling to pieces never attracts a reader. To mend these books you need basic materials such as cloth, tape, glue, needle and thread.'

Here are some tips on how to repair or prevent damage caused by borrowers:

- **Corners folded back**   Some people like to remember where they are in a book by folding down the corner of the page. This spoils the book, weakens the page and is annoying for the next person who reads it. Solve this problem by encouraging students to use bookmarks.

- **Damaged covers**   Damage to the book cover will weaken the book and pages will fall out. Use a dust jacket (you can make these yourself using strong paper or sticky-back plastic) and strengthen weak areas with strong tape. Explain to students that bending a book's spine will cause it to snap just like a bone.

- **Lost pages**   If you cannot find the missing pages, the book (especially if it is a story book) should be removed from the library. If you find the pages, you could try to stick them back into the book, or even sew them.

- **Sticky pages**   These are caused by readers making dirty finger marks on pages or by eating food as they read. Stickiness can result in the page tearing. Sometimes wiping a damp cloth carefully over the sticky bit will clean up the pages.

Looking after magazines

Magazines may need special care too, but for different reasons. Because they are quite thin and are often arranged in large piles, they can easily be removed without the librarian noticing. One way to stop this is to make a magazine folder, as shown in figure 12.3, or simply secure a long piece of split bamboo down the centre fold of the magazine. This helps stop students from taking magazines out of the library without permission. It is recommended that you do not let students borrow magazines; instead encourage them to read magazines in the library.

Figure 12.3 How to make a strong magazine folder

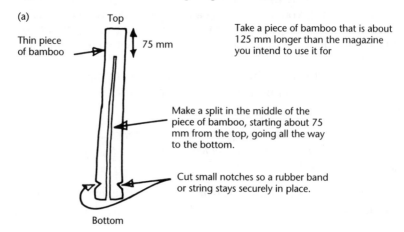

(a)

Top

Thin piece of bamboo →

75 mm

Take a piece of bamboo that is about 125 mm longer than the magazine you intend to use it for

Make a split in the middle of the piece of bamboo, starting about 75 mm from the top, going all the way to the bottom.

Cut small notches so a rubber band or string stays securely in place.

Bottom

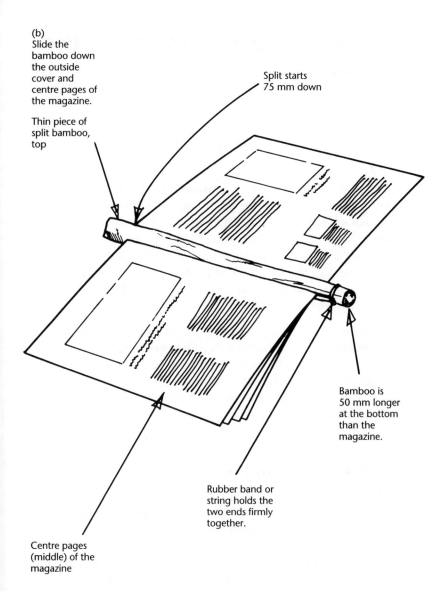

(b)
Slide the bamboo down the outside cover and centre pages of the magazine.

Thin piece of split bamboo, top

Split starts 75 mm down

Bamboo is 50 mm longer at the bottom than the magazine.

Rubber band or string holds the two ends firmly together.

Centre pages (middle) of the magazine

13 Helping students to use the library

What can you do to encourage students to use the library?

The library should be a place students enjoy visiting, so try to make it a friendly place. In the past libraries had many rules. Some librarians even refused to allow students to talk in the library building. These days librarians think that is an unhelpful rule. If students are confused about something let them ask their friends for help first. If they read a book or magazine article they enjoy, let them tell their friends about it. Talking quietly in the library should be allowed, as long as other students are not distracted.

Students must also be taught how to use their library so that they feel confident to find the information they need for their studies. Primary school teachers should make sure children know as much as possible about the library. The roots of a good education are put down at a young age and the same is true for library skills. Encourage children to visit the library and choose their own reading books.

Is the library for enjoyment or study?

The library *is* a place to study, but think for a moment about how you learn best. It is much easier to learn if you are enjoying a subject. Libraries contain information for life. If you show students how a library works whilst they are still at school, then they will continue to use libraries after they leave. They will also be able to help their families and friends to use libraries, not only to find information but also to borrow books to read for pleasure. This is something Nicole Fitton, working in Bangladesh, found that her students did not realise:

'Many students stop using libraries after their studies. They don't see a need for current information or to read for pleasure.'

The key point to remember is that students must understand that the aims of the library are to help their studies and their English reading skills and to provide leisure books. But to achieve these aims you must make the library an enjoyable place. Show students that the library is a lot more than another formroom.

How do you make the library interesting for students?

One of the best ways to attract students to the library is to run three basic 'library tours'. The first will be about books, the second about how the library works and the third involves supervised use of stock in the library.

Before each library tour, plan what you want to say, taking care to keep your message simple. Before you start, estimate how many students will fit into the library. Make sure when you give your library tour that every student will be able to see the things you are pointing out.

If forms at your school are large you may find it helpful to make a taped version of your tour. Students can then borrow this, as Ruth Weitzel recommends in a newsletter for librarians in the Caribbean:

'One way of giving each student an individual tour is to use a cassette tape along with a plan (map) of the library. By following the plan and taped instructions (maybe using a Walkman/personal stereo) a student can explore every corner of the library at their own pace and convenience.'

The book tour

Do your students know much about books? The purpose of this tour is to help students become much more familiar with books. It is usually worth explaining some library terms to them. You could ask each student to find a book and then go through the following points together.

- The book's name, for example *Petals of Blood*, is usually called its **title**.

- The person who wrote the book, Ngugi Wa Thiong'o, is called the **writer** or **author**.

- *Petals of Blood* is a story book. Story books are sometimes called **fiction** books or novels. You can identify a fiction book by its spine label. *Petals of Blood* will have a spine label reading F. T. The F stands for fiction and the T is short for the author's last name, Thiong'o.

- Now ask students the title of the book. Who is the author? Encourage students to point out where the title and author's names are written. These are usually on the **spine**, on the **book jacket** or **front cover** and in the front of the book on the **title page**. If students can learn to identify these parts of the book with no problems, this will be a great help to you.

- Point out the school's name and the **return date label**, which tells students when books that they borrow should be returned to the library.

- Explain that books are fragile. Show students how to turn pages and explain the importance of using bookmarks. Tell students that they should always have clean hands when handling books, and if they borrow a book they must keep it in a clean, dry and safe place.

- Show students an **information** (non-fiction) book. Point out the **contents page**. Explain that it is usually at the front of the book and that it lists the main subjects the book's author has written about. Show students the **index**. Explain that it is usually at the back of the book and that it lists key words and topics alongside a page number. If students then turn to that page, they will find information about the topic.

- Ask how students think they could find what they are looking for in an information book. Listen to their ideas and then prove the usefulness of the contents page. Ask students to work in pairs and use the contents and index pages in your library's information books to find out about a particular topic – flags, for example.

- To finish off the lesson ask the younger children to draw some of the flags they have found. Ask older students to find out when the flag was first designed and some more information about the country.

This will probably be enough information for the students' first library tour. Make sure you ask students if they have any questions. Congratulate them for doing so well and invite them to come back to the library soon.

The 'Get-to-know-the-library' tour
The aim of this tour is to explain how the library works and how students can use it. The following points are recommended as the basis for this tour.

- Explain that books are divided into two main sections: **fiction** and **information** (non-fiction) books. Point out the difference between these books by saying that fiction books are stories and that all other books are for looking up or reading about facts or information about the world.

- Show students where the **bookshelves** are and how books are filed from left to right, top to bottom. All shelves have **shelf guides** taped to them indicating what books are kept on those shelves.

- Take the students to the fiction section. Explain that you must use the alphabet to find your favourite author's book. Tell students that books are arranged in alphabetical order, so that all the books by authors whose last name starts with the same letter (A for example) are kept together. All the books by authors whose last name starts with A will be together and will have a spine label marked F.A. All the books by authors whose last name starts with B will also be kept together and will have a spine label marked F.B; and so on until you reach Z. For tips about teaching alphabetical filing see chapters 9 and 14.

- Hold up a book such as *The Flute* by Chinua Achebe. This should be shelved in the A section because Achebe's last name starts with A. *Quartet* by Rabindranath Tagore would be on the bookshelves with other books by authors whose last name starts with T.

Figure 13.1 A library tour in the Maldives

- Go to the information bookshelves.
  – *If you are using Dewey Decimal Classification* explain that information books are divided (or classified) into subjects and that each subject is given a number. To find a book on a particular subject, students need to know the number of that subject. They should use the subject index pinned to the wall to find this out. For example, if they are looking for a book on religion they will see from the chart that all religious books are given a 200 number.
  – *If you are using Junior Colour Code Classification* explain that information books are divided (or classified) into subjects. Ask students to suggest a favourite subject. If it is sport, then indicate where the sports books are. Point out the wall chart or poster

that shows where to find books on sports. Explain that the coloured labels or stickers make it easier to find the books you want. Check that students understand the system: if books with a purple sticker are for sports information, ask them in which section they would find a book on basketball. They will have to look at the wall chart to find out this – the answer is *all* sports books have a purple spine label and the classification number 700. Make up your own examples from your library's stock.

- Point out that if students want **quick answers** they should go to the **reference** section. These books contain so much information, and are usually so expensive, that libraries do not lend them in case they are lost. Make sure students know how to use a dictionary, an encyclopaedia, etc.

- Say that all fiction books and all information books except those in the reference section can be borrowed. Explain briefly how borrowing works.

- Explain that there is other stock in the library besides books – subject files, project boxes, magazines, audio-visual equipment, etc. Show students where these are and what kinds of information they can expect to find.

- Introduce the library monitors, and perhaps members of the library committee.

- For homework ask the students to pair up and draw a map of the library showing where the stock is kept. Check that students fill in as much information as possible on their map. You could display the best maps on the library wall, perhaps close to the entrance.

The skills tour: using the library
The purpose of this tour is to develop the skills students will need to use the library properly. It follows on from the previous tour. Tell students to work in pairs with the map they made at the end of the last tour.

- Ask students to go and find:
  – a news story in *Time* magazine about a pop group, e.g. UB40
  – a quick answer about the type of bean chocolate is made from (this should be from an encyclopaedia in the reference section)
  – the fiction book *Aditi and the One-Eyed Monkey* by Suniti Namjeshi (if you do not have this book choose one of your favourite books in the fiction section).

- Once you know students can find their way round the library, devise a treasure hunt and play the Treasure Hunt Game (see opposite page).

Treasure Hunt

Tell students to find a particular page in a book, say page 8 of *African Lullaby (Folk Tales from Zimbabwe)* by Chisiya. When they find that page they will also find a clue card (made by you) telling them to go to, say, page 91 of the Thesaurus (kept in the reference section). Each clue card will direct students to another book. This is a very good way of introducing the title catalogue.

Watch out for surprises:

*'One activity was a cause of unexpected excitement. Students had to use the subject index and then find books in a given subject area, which they did quite happily – and brought me the book and the **catalogue card**!'*
Donna Wyness, working with colleagues Finau Laukau and 'Ana Moimoi at Vava'u High School, Tonga

- If you find title catalogue cards are being removed from your index box you could make a hole in the centre of each card and then put a thin stick or rod through all the cards.

- Always encourage students to ask questions. If you see some students are having problems understanding the school library, explain again. Try to give them a special lesson which involves learning by doing. Students learn faster if they have to do things (you could make up a personal treasure hunt to help a student with particular difficulties).

- Encourage students to help each other find books. If a student still has problems, think of a new and simpler way of explaining how the library works.

How to use signs and posters in the library

Putting up signs around the library will help people to use it and will also make the library look more interesting.

Information shelf guides
These signs tell people which books are on each shelf. Draw them in neat letters and pin them (with drawing pins) above the correct shelves, e.g. history, English, business studies, craft, science. Look back at figure 10.2 in chapter 10 for an example.

Skill level guides
If your students have very different levels of ability in English, try to grade all fiction books and use coloured stickers to show the different levels. At a primary school, or for a formroom library, you

could use red for 'beginning to read', yellow for 'moving on' and blue for 'longer stories'. Put up a sign showing what the colours mean. This will help students choose the right book for their age and skill level. The descriptions you choose are very important. Terms such as 'beginning to read', 'moving on' and 'longer stories' encourage children much more than subjective terms such as 'easy' and 'difficult'. A book is not easy for a beginner reader, it is only easy for a literate adult. You could put some of the simpler reading books into a browser box (see chapter 3) to encourage children to decide which book they would like to read.

At secondary schools you might have decided to use colour coding for subject classification, so we recommend that you do not use colour coding for skill level markers as well.

Library opening times
A sign or poster showing clearly when the library is open and when it is closed encourages people to come at the right time and avoids disappointment. This could also be combined with a friendly 'Welcome to the library' sign, like the one shown in the photograph.

Figure 13.2 The library is open, Zanzibar

Library rules

Other very useful signs to make and display in the library are rules and tips on, for example, how to treat books well, how to borrow books, etc.

How else can you attract students to the library?

Make the library look attractive

There are many ways to make the library a pleasant place to visit. Here are some ideas:

- paint it

- hang curtains at the windows

- have fresh flowers or plants on the librarian's table

- put up colourful displays

- make comfortable places for students to sit and read (for pleasure rather than for study).

Some of these may prove difficult, but *all* of them will encourage students to enjoy going to the library.

Hold regular library activities

Encourage students to become involved with the library. One way to do this is to start a library club to help train student librarians and to give you some help running the library and preparing, returning and mending books.

'Without this (help) running the school library is a mammoth and impossible task for one person. If your students are actively involved in such work they will naturally take a pride in the library, and feel it is their library.'
Chris Lane, Kenya

· ·

Teaching tip *Hold fun activities for library club members to help them get to know the stock. One method is to introduce new books, and types of books (e.g. crime stories), by reading an exciting section or chapter. When you have finished reading, ask a few questions about the content to check that students have understood the action. Find out if students liked the story. If they did, tell them where to find similar books.*

If you find this encourages students to read more, you may decide to arrange your fiction books by type of book or genre. Many librarians organise some fiction books into separate sections, for instance:

- *crime writers*
- *thrillers*
- *historical novels*
- *family sagas*
- *animal stories*
- *ghost stories*
- *mysteries*
- *romance.*

The advantage of this system is that if some students like a particular type of book, perhaps a romance, they will be able to find others of the same type. This is something students cannot do if fiction is arranged alphabetically by the author's last name. Note that if you decide to divide fiction books into genres, you will first need to read all the fiction books so that you can put them into the correct section.

Encourage suggestions

Have a suggestions book in the library and encourage students to write down their ideas. Ask teachers if they and their forms will organise regular exhibitions for the library.

Display students' work

Ask teachers to pass on excellent formwork, poems and paintings to you. Then stick them on to large sheets of coloured paper and put them up with drawing pins to make a colourful wall display around the library. Ask students to help you display their work. You could give a prize for the best display. Try to co-ordinate major formroom topics with displays of students' work in the library. Never leave the same work displayed for a long time as it might become torn and dirty.

14 Improving students' library skills

What is the point of improving students' library skills?

For teachers and students to benefit from the library they need experience of using the stock. A good way to provide practical experience is to use games and projects to explain different ways of finding information. This helps students remember library information and it will be fun.

Why are games and projects useful?

Games and projects are useful because they help build literacy skills. This increases students' confidence which makes visiting the library more enjoyable for them. Many of the ideas in this chapter can be used for both primary and secondary school students.

How do you start?

First, make sure you give students their personalised library tour. There are lots of ideas in chapter 13. The projects and exercises in this chapter are for form work, team work and to encourage individual study. You may find it useful to give the winners a small prize to help encourage students to join in these library activities.

Some ideas for games and projects

Making and using bookmarks
The aim of a bookmark is to help students remember where they have read up to. It also encourages students not to spoil books by bending book corners to mark the page they have reached.

Give students pieces of stiff card, cut to about 20 x 5 cm (8 x 2 inches), and ask them to decorate them. You might give a prize for the best one.

Remind students to put their names and form name/number on the bookmark. Any student short of design ideas should be encouraged to draw people, or places, or a favourite sport, or a popular saying.

Using the noticeboard

Ask the library club or teachers to help you organise a group willing to decorate the noticeboard regularly. Change the displays two or three times a term.

Help students find decorations for the noticeboard. Colourful posters are often available from companies, non-government organisations (NGOs), visitors, travel shops, hotels, embassies, high commissions and tourist offices.

Creating a cultural corner

Keep a table free for students to put local objects (or special objects from other countries) on display. Shells, different kinds of money, jewellery, etc. will look attractive and should raise the students' interest in the world outside their school.

My world

Newspaper cuttings about the successes of people students know could be pinned up. When you read the newspapers or local magazines look out for information about students' families, events in nearby villages or the region. This will help you to encourage students to read and become familiar with the newspaper and magazine stock in the library.

Some story telling ideas

There are several ideas here to encourage reading and story telling.

Student book reviews

Encourage students to write short book reviews in an exercise book. Keep the reviews close to the fiction shelf so that other students can look them up and see which stories their friends think are interesting to read.

Start a story

Ask a student to summarise the first chapter of a story book. (This could be done with several students if they wanted to act it out.) Then hold up the book, so everyone can see what the cover looks like, and ask students to guess how the story ends.

Top 10

Grade fiction books into a 'Top 10' at the end of term by asking students to vote for their favourite library book.

Make your own book

Encourage students to produce their own books. The best ones should be kept in the library for everyone to enjoy reading.

Teaching tip *Always remember to check that students understand. Here are two ways of doing this.*

> • ***Comprehension cards*** *You can keep a few multiple-choice question cards which ask questions about a particular fiction book. Although this is a good way for you to find out if the student has understood the story, it is a potentially tedious exercise for the student. It might even make the student start to dislike reading if there is always a test at the end of each book. So use this activity only on an occasional basis.*

> • ***Team worksheets*** *These can be devised for and answered by small groups of students. The team which finishes first is the winner.*

Make imaginative displays

New-book shelf

Make sure the students know when any new fiction or information books are given to the library. Display any new books on a separate shelf. Try to make the display look exciting by adding something which is in the title (e.g. a soccer ball, if it is a about a small girl who starts to play soccer) as well as the actual book(s).

Figure 14.1 A book display, Zanzibar

Theme shelves

To attract reluctant readers you could put some books with similar stories on to separate shelves. Popular themes include mystery, murder and romance.

Local authors

Are there any famous writers in your country? Put together a display of their books and a photograph of the author too if you can find one. Ask local bookshops to help you, or better still ask the author. If you are lucky the author may come and visit the school to read from their book, or talk about their work.

Theme tables

A theme table is similar to a cultural corner; the difference is that the theme table display should focus on just one aspect of life. Ask students (forms or the library club) to collect pieces of interesting information (e.g. objects, poems and stories) about one particular subject or theme. Some themes that have proved successful are holidays, homes, the environment, animals, the night sky, town and village life.

Tree of Knowledge posters

These are very good for showing students which subject area they should go to to find the information they want. Use a Tree of Knowledge poster to display a subject index checklist showing how your library's classification system is organised (for more about this see chapter 7). Make a colourful poster like the one shown in figure 14.2 and pin it up on the wall.

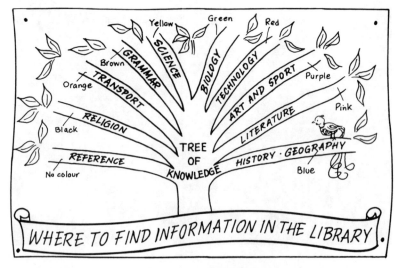

Figure 14.2 The Tree of Knowledge explains the classification system

Mobiles

Mobiles are another useful way of displaying information. For
instance, if a student is having problems finding out about
groundnuts for agricultural or science studies, suggest small groups
of students draw a variety of locally grown crops. Then divide the
students into pairs or threes and ask them to cut out their pictures.
With the teacher–librarian's help, the students then identify which
classification section each picture belongs to. Next ask the students
to add the correct classification number on to their picture(s).
Finally, make the pictures into a mobile and hang it from a high
point in the room. This will give students a quick reminder about
where they can find information about agriculture, and will also
serve to decorate the library. Mobiles can of course be made using
pictures from a variety of favourite subject areas.

Organise library events

Holding special events is an excellent way of encouraging students
to make more use of the library. Here are some ideas.

A readathon

This is a fun reading competition. It is most successful with
secondary school students and fairly confident readers. The aim is
to see how long a form can keep reading a story book out loud.
Students take it in turns to read, each reading one page. Give a
prize to the form that reads the most pages. Encourage all
competitors to vote for the student who reads in the most
interesting way.

Story hour

Younger children always enjoy listening to stories. If the story is
particularly good, then this can be an excellent activity for
secondary school students too. Encourage students to sit
themselves comfortably and then read the story to them. You
might like to do this under a shady tree, or even at night. The
teacher–librarian should prepare for story hour by reading the
book (or chapter) in advance. It is important to use your
imagination when you read and to try to make the characters
come alive: use different-sounding voices when a new person or
animal 'speaks'. If you enjoy singing there is sure to be a chance
for you to sing parts of the story too!

Current events

Read a short passage or news item from an international magazine
such as *Newsweek* or a magazine published in your area. Then ask
students to talk about what it means for them, their country and
the world. This is especially useful for secondary school students.

More games to teach library skills

Authors game
Tell everyone in the form to pretend to be an author. First they can think up a title for their book. Then, on a large piece of paper, help students draw an imaginary book cover for their pretend book, including their own name as the author. Finally, all the students pretend to be books and line themselves up in alphabetical order.

Jigsaw
Ask pairs of students to draw large maps of the library, showing where the stock is being kept. Their maps should include fiction, non-fiction and reference books, magazines, noticeboards, etc. When the maps are finished ask the students to cut them up into ten large pieces. Each pair then muddles up the pieces and swops with another pair. Who puts the jigsaw together the fastest?

General knowledge quiz
Quizzes are excellent for secondary school students. A library quiz should test students' knowledge of what is available in the library and develop their library skills. Quizzes encourage students to use a variety of information stock – dictionary, atlas, magazines, encyclopaedia – as well as rehearse library rules and match up specific subjects with their classification labels.

Set ten questions, the answers to which can be found in the books and stock in the library. Figure 14.3 shows an example of the sort of questions you might set. Give students two or three weeks to find the answers. Then, when all the students are together, perhaps at assembly or at an end-of-term party, you can announce the names of the students who found all the correct answers. If you have a small prize, then put those names into a container and ask one of the other students to pull out the name of the winner.

'Regular competitions have encouraged students to understand how to use a library properly and students and teachers alike were increasingly making use of the facilities, with well over 50 per cent of students having a book out at any one time.'
Simon Etherton, running a library at Allardyce Secondary School, Solomon Islands, with the help of 12 student monitors including Stephen Kapu and Nester Haiptu

1 What does 'sustainable' mean?

2 Put these words in the order they appear in
the dictionary:
excuse, examination, extra, expel.

3 What colour spine label or classification
number would you find on a book about
volcanoes?

4 Where are books on bee keeping kept in the
library?

5 What is the capital city of Vietnam?

6 Which countries share a border with
Uganda?

7 What was the main story in *Time* magazine
[put issue number and date].

8 How many players are needed for a rugby
union team?

9 Looking at the display about turtles [use
your own library display] name the nearest
turtle nesting beach to the school.

10 What happens if you lose a library book?

Figure 14.3 Sample general knowledge questions for a library quiz

15 Library checklists and routines

Why have checklists?

A checklist is a list of essential tasks. Setting up a library involves a number of tasks and it can be easy to forget to do them all or to do them in the recommended order. A checklist helps to remind you what you need to do to set up a library and in what order to do it.

Why have routines?

A routine is a task you do regularly. Establishing a set of library routines will help you and student helpers to remember to do all the essential tasks in the library, such as putting books back on shelves and checking all books are returned by the specified date. The teacher–librarian, students (library monitors and club members), staff and the library committee should all be involved with library routines. Some of these tasks will need to be performed daily, some weekly, some fortnightly (every two weeks) and some at the end of every term. Routines ensure that the library is well organised and well maintained.

How to set up checklists for your library

First you must plan what you need to do, step-by-step. Make sure your plan is logical and that it involves students and staff. Then write down lists of tasks in the order in which they need to be done. Three model checklists are given below.

Before opening the library

1 Organise a library committee and decide on library rules, opening times, staffing and the amount of help you need from library monitors.

2 Decide on the method of lending books and how to classify information (non-fiction) books.

3 Prepare the library room, make the bookshelves and organise equipment and stationery.

4 Check that the library is secure.

5 Get to know the different types of library stock and parts of a book. If you already have a library you may want to remove damaged or inappropriate stock.

6   Make an accession register. Glue the school nameplate and, depending on your lending method, a return date label into all books.

7   Divide books into fiction and information (non-fiction). Give all fiction books a spine label. Divide information books into subject areas according to your chosen method of classification. Give each information book a spine label.

8   Make library catalogues. This will include a shelf list and title catalogue.

9   Put books on to shelves. Information books are arranged by subject. Fiction books are arranged in alphabetical order by the author's last name.

10 Make shelf guides so that books can be found easily. Put up a subject index and posters on the walls to make the library more attractive and to remind students of any rules about using or borrowing books.

11 Make sure that your lending system is fully operational, so that records can be kept of who has borrowed which books.

Opening the library
1   Give form tours to all students and teachers when your library first opens, and to all new students and teachers thereafter.

2   Remember to explain
    • the parts of the book
    • how to care for books
    • where to find information and fiction books
    • any rules, especially about borrowing books.

Improving the library
1   Organise library displays.

2   Set regular competitions.

3   Order more books and other stock (see chapter 16).

Recommended routines for your library

Daily routine
1   Ensure the library is open at the times you have told everyone.

2   Let students borrow books.

3   Put returned books back on the shelves.

4   Dust the shelves and sweep the floor.

Beginning of day
- Change the date stamp.

End of day
- Lock up money, lockable cupboards and the door.

Weekly routine

1   Check which students have borrowed books that have passed their return date. Ask library monitors to remind students to return their books.

2   Especially at the start of the school year and when you first set up the library, organise form visits to the library (see chapter 13).

3   Repair books.

Fortnightly routine

1   Change new books or formroom displays.

2   Organise competitions or library games.

3   If you have ordered books, check when they will arrive at the library. When they arrive, add them to the accession register.

New books routine

1   Add every new book to the accession register and give it an accession number.

2   Glue in the school nameplate.

3   Decide if the book is fiction or information (non-fiction).

Fiction books

1   Decide where the book should be filed in the fiction section. Sort books into skill levels if you are setting up a library at a primary school or a formroom library.

2   Mark the spine of the book with an F for fiction and the first letter of the author's last name.

3   Add the book to the shelf list and title catalogue.

4   Tell students about the new book.

5   Put the book on the shelves.

Information (non-fiction) books

1   Decide which subject each book is about.

2   Classify it in the appropriate section.

3   Mark the spine of the book with a classification label.

4   Make a shelf list and a title card for the new book.

5   Tell students about the new book and make a display.

6   Put the book on the shelves.

Damaged books routine
Books may be damaged while they are on loan. If you see any books with torn covers, spines which need to be glued or loose pages, put them on one side and repair them when you have time. If you cannot make repairs, the book should be withdrawn from the library stock.

End-of-term routine
1   Clean the library very well. Use insect sprays.

2   Ask for all books to be returned to the library. At the end of each school year you may like to organise a stocktake (see chapter 8).

3   Make a list of missing books and try to find them. If you cannot find a book it should be withdrawn from stock. This means crossing it out of the accession register and removing it from the shelf list and title catalogue.

4   Check your books to see they are all appropriate. Any out-of-date or damaged books should be removed from the library.

5   Thank library monitors (or club members) for their help.

6   Remember to ask if anyone has any ideas on how to make the library even better.

16 Increasing your library stock

● ●

How can you find more stock for your library?

The best way of increasing your library collection is to ask as many
people as possible for more stock. Local families, business people
and former pupils are often keen to help schools improve their
library. You can also request free books by writing letters to donor
agencies or by inviting officials to visit your school, so that you
can explain your plans for the library.

If people are unable to donate books, or gift books are the wrong
level for students, you should consider buying books. This can be
done at local bookshops or by using a catalogue supplied by
overseas companies. You may need to prove to your school's head
teacher that the library needs a bigger book-buying budget, or you
may need to fundraise. It is recommended that you organise
fundraising locally before approaching aid organisations.

Where can you get free books for your library?

Donated books are free. Some may have been used by people in
other countries, before they are given to your library, but this is
not a problem if the books are in good condition.

If you know what types of books your library needs, write a letter
on headed paper explaining to the potential donor, or aid
organisation, exactly what books you need.

Your letter should include details of:

• the number of pupils at the school
• the students' level of education and reading abilities
• whether you need multiple copies (for form lessons)
• whether the books are for a formroom or school library
• any titles you particularly need, e.g. textbooks.

The letter should be signed by two people, the teacher–librarian
and the head teacher, for example. Remember to keep a copy of
the letter as you may have to wait a long time for an answer.

Try writing to the following organisations for more information
about getting free books for your library.

Book Aid International

Book Aid International (formerly Ranfurly Library Service) sends out more than 700,000 books a year in its work supporting education and literacy in less developed countries. The best way to find out if your school is eligible for books is to write a detailed letter to BAI.

If BAI can provide books for your school you will receive some more information about the scheme, as well as a project proposal and a book requirements form. Both these forms need to be filled in before books can be sent to your school.

To help BAI improve its service it is important to write and say how useful staff and students have found the books. This information may also be used by the organisation to help people in Britain know more about the need for books in countries like your own.

- Book Aid International, 2 Coldharbour Place, 39/41 Coldharbour Lane, Camberwell, London SE5 9NR, UK.

The Asia Foundation

The Asia Foundation is an American organisation which sometimes sends free books to schools. Write to its headquarters at this address:

- Asia Foundation, 465 California Street, San Francisco, CA 94104, USA.

Peace Corps

Peace Corps is an American volunteer agency that sometimes supplies equipment like books for school libraries. Write directly to the Peace Corps office in your country.

Embassies and High Commissions

Write to the High Commissioner at the office in your country.

International Book Bank

International Book Bank (IBB) is one of the largest book-sending agencies in the world. It has offices in Canada and USA. If you want to make use of IBB's services write a letter (on headed paper and signed by two members of staff) explaining what sort of books you want for your school and the number and educational standard of the students.

- International Book Bank Inc, 608 L Folcroft Street, Baltimore, Maryland, 21224, USA.

The British Council

The British Council has offices in many countries and its staff can offer free advice about setting up a library. They can also tell you if there is a policy for donating books or giving grants for books to schools in your country. Although the British Council does supply some books these are usually suitable for post-graduate study only.

Churches

Many churches and NGOs publish picture and reading books which students may enjoy. Some may also run bookshops in your country and be willing to donate stock.

As well as writing to these organisations, you could also invite Embassy Officials, High Commissioners or aid donors to visit your school. But make sure you discuss this with the head teacher and other staff before you send an invitation.

Why must gift books be checked carefully?

The books that will be most useful for the students and teachers at your school will be books which are interesting, appropriate and in good condition. Assess each book carefully (using the suggestions in chapter 5) and decide if people at the school will enjoy using it and/or if they will find it useful for their studies.

Some schools have good experiences when they are sent gift books and some have bad experiences. This is what Peter Williams, working with Tony Dadalo at University of South Pacific Library, Solomon Islands, found:

'The library has lots of books but most are irrelevant to the courses being run. The books we get via aid rarely suit our needs.'

However, the chief librarian at Bulawayo Public Library, Zimbabwe, has a different story:

'Almost all the books Ranfurly Library Service (now called BAI) sent are unavailable here. The consignment represents almost half our total book needs for the year. . . Book supply here has continued to deteriorate, with the local currency having been devalued by over 20 per cent in the last three months. A £10 book now costs $100 in local shops compared with only $10 a few years ago. The Zimbabwean dollar used to be worth £1, now it is only worth 15p!'

Where can you buy stock for your library?

If you are going to buy books the first place to look is in bookshops in your country. You should visit these with other teachers to help you select appropriate books. If you do not know which books you want, a useful source of information is the National Library. Wherever possible you should liaise with the National Library and read their review journals.

Library suppliers

You could also try contacting library suppliers. These are businesses that specialise in selecting and supplying books to libraries. Some offer free catalogues and others can recommend useful titles for your school library.

- Morley Books, Elmfield Road, Morley, Leeds LS27 0NN, UK. Tel: (+44) 532 538811. Fax: (+44) 532 527925.

  Morley Books will send a free catalogue. Inside you can find details about books, videos and audio-cassettes, plus book jackets, catalogue cards, date stamps and reinforced book bindings.

- James Askew & Son Ltd, 218–222 North Road, Preston, Lancashire PR1 1SY, UK. Tel: (+44) 772 555947. Fax: (+44) 772 254860.

  James Askew has a free catalogue which gives details of books and school/college textbooks. The company has a stockroom holding at least a million books. If you want shelf-ready books the company can provide this service, supplying book jackets, date labels, spine labels and rubber stamps.

- Burchell & Martin Ltd, 34 Granville Street, Birmingham B1 2LJ, UK. Tel: (+44) 21 643 1888. Fax: (+44) 21 631 3492.

  Burchell & Martin offers a different service. Instead of sending out catalogues, they ask potential customers to provide details about the school and about the subjects staff and students are interested in. From this information they make a free list of recommended books and audio-visual material, that will be suitable for your school library. You can then order any of these, as well as book jackets, bindings, plastic laminated covers and book cards.

Books by local authors

It can be difficult to obtain books written by local writers or authors from neighbouring countries. If the books you want are not available locally try writing to overseas library suppliers or publishers for their catalogue. These are usually free. One example is the **African Books Collective Ltd**. This is a non-profit-making organisation which was set up in the UK. It has a large catalogue of creative writing by African authors. The catalogue is free and includes an order form. All orders must be sent with full payment, including postage and packing. The address to write to is:

- African Books Collective Ltd, The Jam Factory, 27 Park End Street, Oxford OX1 1HU, UK.

  If you want to know more about books published in your country you could try writing to **IBBY**, the **International Board on Books for Young People**. There are IBBY branches throughout the world, including Chile, Mexico, Eastern Europe and India. For more details about your nearest IBBY member's address, contact the head office in Switzerland:

- International Board on Books for Young People, Nonnenweg 12, Postfach CH 4003, Basel, Switzerland.

Specialist books

The following organisations have books on more specialist subjects. You could write to them for free catalogues or more details about what they publish. **Save the Children Fund (SCF)** is well-known for its health and nutritional work in many countries. However, it also publishes some books for schools, as well as teachers' handbooks. Write to them for a free catalogue at this address:

- Save the Children Fund, Education Unit, 17 Grove Lane, London SE5 8RD, UK.

The **Islamic Foundation** produces some interesting books for children and students, for example *Muslim Nursery Rhymes* by Mustafa Yusuf McDermott. For a full list of books write to:

- Islamic Foundation, The Sales Manager, Unit 9, The Old Dunlop Factory, 62 Evington Valley Road, Leicester LE5 5LJ, UK.

VSO (Voluntary Service Overseas) has its own book publishing programme, which produces practical texts for the developing world, known as 'The ECOE Programme'. Titles range from *Agriculture and Natural Resources* to *The Science Teachers' Handbook*. For details of the programme write to:

- The ECOE Programme, VSO, 317 Putney Bridge Road, London SW15 2PN, UK.

Some excellent appropriate technology books are available from **Intermediate Technology Publications**. For your free catalogue, which lists many books offering practical advice, write to:

- Intermediate Technology Publications, 103–105 Southampton Row, London WC1B 4HH, UK.

A group that specialises in health topics and ideas to help children learn is the **Teaching Aids At Low Cost (TALC)** programme. Popular publications include the *Child-to-Child* readers. Write for details of titles and prices to:

- TALC, PO Box 49, St Albans, Hertfordshire AL1 4AX, UK.

How to solve coupon payment problems

Some aid agencies (e.g. UNESCO) that fund schools supply them with coupons rather than cheques or cash. If you are having difficulties exchanging your UNESCO coupons for books for the library you should contact UNESCO at its headquarters in Paris:

- UNESCO, 1 Place de Fontenoy, 75700 Paris, France.

How do you choose books from a catalogue?

The answer to this question will depend on your budget and on which books students and staff need. It is best to choose books with a colleague, asking the advice of teachers in different subjects or members of the library committee. This is how Renato Masetti, working at Dreger Hagen Secondary School, Papua New Guinea with Elizabeth Bart, selected stock:

'We sat down with all the catalogues and chose books we thought would be good. We were setting up our own library so we went for big, hardbacked books, like encyclopaedias that would last a long time.'

Note, however, that protective plastic dust jackets (from library suppliers, or made by yourself from strong paper) can ensure paperback books have as long a life as hardback books.

How do you order books?

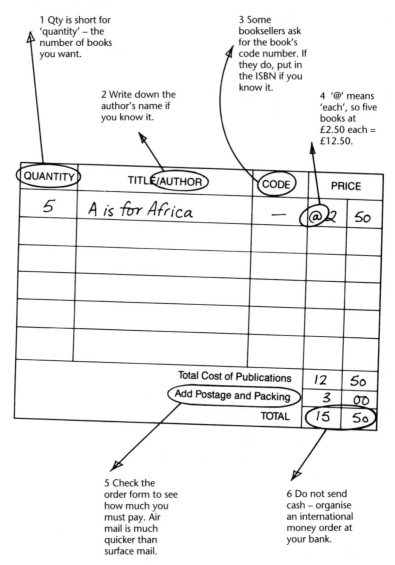

Figure 16.1 How to complete an order form for books

When you have decided which books the library needs and the school can afford, you will need to complete the order form. Figure 16.1 explains how to do this. Then you must send your order off. This will probably involve going to a bank and asking for an international money order or a banker's draft. If you have not done this before, ask the school accountant or a bank clerk to help.

It is important to keep a record of books you have ordered. You can do this using an exercise book, as shown in figure 16.2.

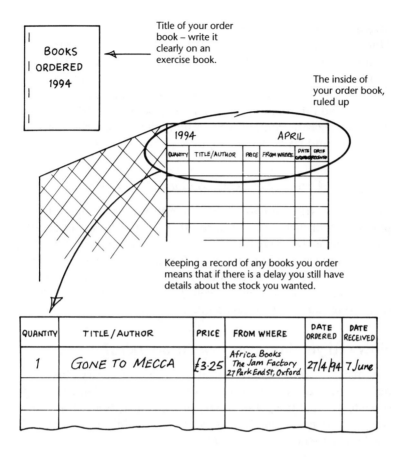

Figure 16.2 How to keep a record of books you have ordered

Where can you get magazines for the library?
You may find your school is already being sent some free magazines and newspapers. If you are not on a mailing list, try asking the chief librarian or library assistant at the public library if they can help you organise some magazines to be sent to your school.

Magazine subscription services
You can also order magazines from two subscription services – **Periodical Subscription Service** and **Dawson's International Journal Subscription Service**.

• Periodical Subscription Service, B H Blackwell Ltd, Broad Street, Oxford OX1 3BQ, UK.

• Dawson's International Journal Subscription Service, Cannon House, Folkestone, Kent, UK.

Magazines spread ideas

Link-Up is a magazine which is sent out four times a year to librarians around the world. It was set up in 1988 by VSO, UNAIS (United Nations Association International Service) and CUSO volunteer librarians who have worked with counterparts in libraries and information centres in developing countries. You may find the magazine contains some useful ideas, so ask the editors, Gill Harris and David Membrey, to send free copies to you. The address is:

• *Link-Up*, 64 Ennersdale Road, London SE13 5JD, UK.

Anyone can write for *Link-Up*. This might be a good chance to publicise your successes and warn other teacher–librarians about any problems they may have to face when setting up and running a school library. Send in a report or feature story of between 500 and 1000 words. If you have any photographs or drawings of your school library enclose them as well. These will be returned if you write your name and address on them clearly.

How can you improve *your* library skills?

You may find your local technical college or university offers residential or distance education courses in library skills. The best place to ask is at the public library or the centre itself. Most courses suggest students should have a recognised qualification in English and/or experience of running a library.

One overseas correspondence course (which you can study at home and/or at the school where you are working) is the City & Guilds 737 Open Learning Certificate in Library and Information Competencies at Telford College. You study for one year and take five exams, as well as arranging for a chartered (professionally qualified) librarian to supervise some practical tasks. In 1993 the course cost about £300. For more information write to Donald Steele or Maggie Young at:

• Telford College, Crewe Toll, Edinburgh EH4 2NZ, Scotland, UK.

The International Federation of Library Associates and Institutions (IFLA) offers a wide range of help for libraries in the developing world. This includes scholarships for in-service training, a publications programme, the establishment of community information/resource centres and literacy work. IFLA has offices around the world. For details of the one closest to you and more about IFLA's work write to:

• IFLA Headquarters, PO Box 95312, 2509 CH The Hague, The Netherlands, Europe.

Appendix 1 Junior Colour Code classification schedule

● ●

The Junior Colour Code, which is an adaptation of the Dewey Decimal Classification scheme, is printed here to help you classify books for your school library. The ten main sections are the same as the Dewey system, although it is recommended that you divide science books into two main classifications (500 for general science books and 570 for biology books). To use the JCC system you need to identify which main section a book belongs to and then mark its spine with its classification number and a coloured label. For more information see chapter 7.

000	**Reference**	304	Acid rain	355	Weapons
(no colour)		304	Pollution	356	Army
001	Signs	305	Nomads	358	Air force
004	Computers	305	Travellers	359	Navy
020	Libraries	306	Death	361	Charities
030	Dictionaries	306	Families	362	Adoption
030	Encyclopaedias	306	Sexism	362	Elderly persons
060	Museums	307	Cities	362.5	Child abuse
070	Newspapers	307	Communities	363	Disasters
		307	Town life	363	Fire service
100	**Philosophy**	307	Village life	363	Lifeboats
(black colour)		320	Apartheid	363	Road safety
		320	Racism	363	Water safety
200	**Religions**	323.4	Civil rights	364	Crime
(black colour)		325	Immigration	364	Pirates
220	Bible	326	Slavery	364	Spies
221	Old Testament	331	Careers	365	Prisons
225	New Testament	331	Trade unions	370	Education
230	Christianity	331	Unemployment	370	Schools
232	Christmas	332	Banks	380	Communi-
232	Easter	332	Money		cations
232	Jesus Christ	338	Factories	380	Transport
293	Buddhism	339	Poverty	383	Post Office
295	Hinduism	340	Law	383	Stamps
296	Judaism	341	European	384	Telephones
296	Talmud		Community	385	Railways
296	Torah	341	United Nations	386	Canals
297	Islam	350	Government	386	Boats
297	Koran	350	Local	386	Harbours
297	Muhammad		government	386	Sea
297	Qur'an	350	Parliament	386	Ships
298	Rastafarianism	351	Police	386	Submarines
		355	Arms and	388	Bicycles
300	**Transport and**		armour	388	Buses
	Economics	355	Guns	388	Cars
(orange colour)		355	Nuclear warfare	388	Cycling
302	Media	355	War	388	Motor cycles

Appendix 2   The VSO ECOE Programme

●●

Evaluating and Communicating our Overseas Experience

The need

Over the past 35 years more than 20,000 volunteers have worked overseas with VSO. Currently, there are over 1700 volunteers working in over 50 countries in Africa, Asia, the Pacific and the Caribbean for periods of two years or more. We have become increasingly aware that much of this valuable experience has not been recorded in ways which make it accessible and communicable. The ECOE Programme addresses this need.

The aim

The aim is to record volunteers' professional experience in books, reports, videos, seminars and conferences. This body of knowledge supplements and supports the work of individual volunteers. It also provides information which is accessible not only to volunteers but also to their employers overseas and to other agencies for whom the information is relevant. Care is taken to present each area of volunteer experience in the context of current thinking about development so that VSO both contributes to development discussions and learns lessons from them for the continuance of its work.

Advisory panel

A panel of opinion leaders in relevant professions and development thinking advises on the selection and commissioning of ECOE publications. For further information write to:

* The ECOE Programme Manager, VSO, 317 Putney Bridge Road, London SW15 2PN, UK. Telephone (+44) 081 780 2266. Fax: (+44) 081 780 1326.

Publications

Agriculture and natural resources – A manual for development workers
Penelope Amerena
118pp   1990   VSO   ISBN: 0 9509 0503 8   £9.95(excl. p+p)

Children actively learning – The New Approach to Primary Education in Bhutan
Peter Collister and Michael Etherton
58pp   1991   VSO/ITP   ISBN: 1 85339 111 5   £4.95 (excl. p+p)

Culture, cash and housing – Community and tradition in low-income building
Maurice Mitchell and Andy Bevan
130pp   1992   VSO/ITP   ISBN: 1 85339 153 0   £6.95 (excl. p+p)

Introductory technology – A teacher's resource book
Adrian Owens
142pp   1990   VSO/ITP   ISBN: 1 85339 064 X   £9.95 (excl. p+p)

Made in Africa – Learning from carpentry hand-tool projects
Janet Leek, Andrew Scott and Matthew Taylor
70pp   1993   VSO/ITP   ISBN: 1 85339 214 6   £4.95 (excl. p+p)

Using technical skills in community development
Jonathan Dawson, edited by Mog Ball
64pp   1990   VSO/ITP   ISBN: 1 85339 078 X   £4.95 (excl. p+p)

Water supplies for rural communities
Colin and Mog Ball
64pp   1992   VSO/ITP   ISBN: 1 85339 112 3   £5.95 (excl. p+p)

To order these titles and for more information contact the ECOE Programme Manager, VSO, 317 Putney Bridge Road, London, UK. Telephone (+44) 081 780 2266. Fax: (+44) 081 780 1326.

Key words

Accession number   A unique number given to each library book recorded in the **accession register**.

Accession register   A record of books in the order that the library receives them.

Alphabetical order   A way of sorting information into A-to-Z order. Fiction books, for example, are usually organised in alphabetical order by the author's last name.

Atlas   A book of maps.

Audio-visual stock   Items you can listen to (audio) or watch (visual). It includes tapes and videos.

Author   A person who has written a book or an article.

Bar code   A design, usually on the back cover of a book, consisting of numbers and parallel lines which can be read by machines to confirm the price of the book. Bar codes can be found on many different products including books.

Book jacket   A strong paper cover or sticky-back plastic cover that protects a book.

Book pocket   A paper pocket, sometimes called a card pocket, into which an information ticket about a library book can be placed. When the book is borrowed the ticket is removed and stored for easy reference by the librarian. Book pockets are often combined with the school nameplate and **return date label**. They are usually glued on to a page near the front of a book.

Bookend   A heavy object, perhaps a stone or wooden 'L' shape, used to keep books standing upright on bookshelves.

Bookmark   A narrow piece of card which can be put inside a book to remind the reader which page they have reached.

Bookshelf   A flat board in a cupboard, or against a wall, on which books are arranged. Bookshelves can also be a specially made set of shelves. This is the best place to display books and other library stock. It is possible to make temporary bookshelves and book cupboards from a variety of materials, e.g. tea chests.

Borrow   To take away books or other stock, with the librarian's permission, for a set period of time.

Borrower card   A card completed and kept by the librarian which identifies the name of the borrower as well as the book they have borrowed.

Borrowing system   A method which allows people to take books out of the library for a set period of time, for study or leisure reading. A written record of who has borrowed the book helps the teacher–librarian to find the book if it is not returned by the specified date on the **return date label**.

Browser box   A low box, divided into sections, which can be used to display a few books. It is a good way of encouraging reluctant readers to look at the different types of book available in the library and is recommended for primary school students.

Caution fee   Some schools ask parents to pay a caution fee at the start of each term. This is usually refunded if the student does not damage any of the school's property, including library stock.

Classification   A way of dividing information books into coded subject areas. The books are labelled with identifying codes on the **spine**. There are numerous ways of classifying books of which three are described in this book. Read about them in chapter 7.

Contents   This is a list of the subjects covered in a book. It is usually at the front of information books and is a useful way of finding out if the book you are looking through has the information you want.

Copy   In a library, a copy means one book. If you have several books, with the same title and by the same author, then you have multiple copies. Each copy should be given its own unique **accession number.**

Copyright   A legal term which protects writers' work from reproduction for a specific number of years without the permission of the publisher.

Date stamp   A rubber stamp, used with an ink pad, that can be set to a specific date and used on the **return date label**.

Dewey Decimal Classification (Dewey or DDC)   One method of dividing or classifying information books by subject.

Dictionary   A book giving the meaning of words in any one language, arranged in **alphabetical order.**

Display   An attractively arranged group of objects. Displays are used to encourage students to visit the library.

Divider card   Stiff paper used to divide a collection of **index**

cards into easy-to-check sections. They are often a little taller than and/or a different colour from index cards.

Dust jacket   A protective cover for a book, usually make of thick paper or sticky-back plastic.

Encyclopaedia   A reference book where you can find quick answers to all sorts of questions.

Fiction   A type of story that is not based on fact. Types of fiction stories include thrillers, ghost stories, crime, romance, etc.

File   To arrange in a particular order.

Fine   A sum of money imposed as a punishment if borrowed books are brought to the library later than the agreed date stamped or written on the **return date label**.

Flip chart   A poster-size information diagram. These often take a long time to draw, so they should be stored safely in the library, either rolled up or in a **project box**.

Formroom library   A way of organising and keeping books in cupboards in a formroom if the school does not have a separate room for a library.

Front cover   Protective cover of a book. Most have the book's **title** written on them as well as the names of the **author** and **publisher**.

Genre   Fiction books of the same type: for example, many authors specialise in writing one type of book such as mysteries, romance, or thrillers.

Hardback   A book with a strong cover, usually more expensive and not as easily damaged as a **paperback** book.

Index   An alphabetical list of subjects, together with page references, usually found at the back of information books.

Index card   Standard-sized record card with details about each item of library stock, usually arranged in a specific order.

Information book   A book which contains facts, e.g. **textbooks** and **reference books**.

ISBN   An individual number given to each published book, used by book publishers around the world to help identify books. It can be useful to know if you are ordering books from an overseas **library supplier's** catalogue.

Issue box   A container where index cards are filed in a systematic order. It is sometimes called an index box.

Junior Colour Code   A method of dividing or classifying information books by subject.

Junior fiction   Imaginary stories for young children.

Ledger   A large book for writing records down.

Lend   To allow library users to borrow books for a set period of time.

Lending system   See **borrowing system**.

Librarian or teacher–librarian   The person responsible for organising the library. The best teacher–librarians will encourage everyone's interest in the library and share library decisions and duties with a range of people, including **library committee** members, **library club** members and **library monitors**.

Library   A place where books and other stock are kept in an organised way so that it is easy for users to find the information they want.

Library club   A club for students who are interested in learning more about the library and book management.

Library committee   A small decision-making group chosen from the school staff and students.

Library monitor   A student responsible for helping the teacher–**librarian** with library tasks. It is best to make the job of library monitor a privilege.

Library supplier   A company that specialises in providing books, and sometimes stationery and other equipment, for libraries.

Literacy   The ability to read what you want to read and to write what you want to write. Schools, books and libraries aim to develop literacy skills.

Magazine   A thin paper booklet containing very up-to-date information, stories and photographs, published at regular intervals.

Mobile   A hanging display that can be used to show information and to decorate the library.

Novel   A book of **fiction** containing a single story.

Office equipment   Essential apparatus needed for running a library.

Oversize book   A large book that does not fit on to standard size bookshelves.

Pamphlet   A small booklet or handbook that does not have a **spine**.

Paperback   A book with a paper cover.

Periodical   Another name for a **magazine**.

Photograph   A visual information record. Photographs are always popular with students; however, they can be easily damaged or torn so the best place to store them is in a photograph album.

Poster   A large picture, printed or drawn, designed to provide information. Posters can be made by the **library club**, or bought from shops, to decorate the library.

Project box/subject file   A box or file in which a variety of stock about the same subject, e.g. the weather, is kept. A project box is a good place to store **pamphlets** and videos which might not be easy to see on bookshelves.

Publication date   The date when a book is published. It is usually at the front of the book.

Publisher   A company that produces books or **magazines**.

Quarterly   A way of describing something that is done four times a year. Some **magazines**, for example, are published every three months – four times a year.

Readathon   A fun story-telling exercise when a series of students read a book, out loud, for a long time.

Reference book   An information book where students and staff can find quick answers, and which cannot be borrowed from the library.

Reprint   A further edition of a book, produced by the **publisher** when the initial number of copies printed has sold out.

Return date label   A place in the book where the date by which a borrowed book must be returned to the library is written or stamped.

Routine   A task that is done regularly.

Shelf guide   A sign that shows library users where books and stock are kept on the bookshelves.

Shelf list   A complete list of all the books and stock in the library, kept in the same order as the books on the bookshelves.

Silica gel   A substance used to dry the air so that humidity does not damage **audio-visual** equipment.

Skill level   The stage of development a student has reached in their reading ability. Library books can be arranged according to skill levels or degrees of difficulty. One method is to sort primary school books and formroom books into three skill levels, so beginners, better beginners and more advanced readers can easily find the right book for their current skill level.

Spine   The backbone of a book. If the spine is broken the book's pages and cover may fall apart.

Spine label   A label glued to a book's **spine** so that you can quickly identify the subject area of the book and where it should be kept on the bookshelves.

Stationery   Pens, glue, paper, etc.

Sticky-back plastic   Plastic with one sticky side which can be used to give added protection to **book jackets** or covers.

Stock   All items in the library.

Stocktake   A method of checking to see what **stock** is in the library. To make a stocktake you will need a **shelf list**.

Subject catalogue   An alphabetical list of the subjects covered by the books in the library.

Subject index   A checklist of main subjects. Use the subject index to remind students and yourself of the main subjects in the library and their classification codes.

Subscription   Advance payment for a set number of magazines, e.g. for six months or one year. Most subscription offers will save you some money in the long term.

Textbook   A standard book for a particular subject of study.

Theme table   A table used for special displays on one topic. The theme 'What do we find on the beach', for example, might include a map of the local beach, pictures of special seabirds, some shells, dried seaweed, a turtle egg and a project book from one of the classes with short stories and pictures of strange objects students have found on the beach.

Thesaurus   A reference book of related word lists. It can help users increase their vocabulary.

Title   The name of a book.

Title catalogue   All the titles of the books in the library, written down on individual index cards, then filed in alphabetical order.

Title page   The page at the front of a book which has the **title**, **author** and **publisher** printed on it. It is usually a right-hand page and is where you are recommended to glue the school nameplate and **return date label**.

Title verso page   A left-hand page near the front of a book containing information about the book (e.g. publisher, date published, etc.)

Index

•••

Note: page numbers in *italic* include photographs and illustrations